BINGHAMTON NEW YORK

Home Is Where My Heart Is

Written by David A. Bogart

DEDICATION

I am dedicating this book to all the people who came here with a dream. They came here to prosper and felt strongly that this city was a great place to raise a family and build their business. The employers who started their business here only became some of the most influential companies in the United States today. They came with their dreams and followed through with them to fruition.

They cared about their workers and the people living in our area. There are signs of their love for people and children all over our city—different things left for us to enjoy to this day.

The love these people had for Binghamton has trickled down to a nucleus of others that would never think of leaving this area. It is a feeling of carrying on their thoughts and dreams within our future within our own families. It affected me, and I am one of those people. I always felt it was vital for me to stay here and not dwell on any negatives, but to maintain and try my best to improve the positives.

This book will help bring Binghamton back to the status that these people formed long ago. Although Binghamton is no longer what it once was, we still maintain the philosophy from the ones before us. We are a dynamic city. A city that is always trying to improve in any area that we can.

COPYRIGHT PAGE

Author of the book: David A. Bogart

Book title: HOME Is Where My Heart Is

Copyright© 2021, David A. Bogart

ISBN-9798507909384

Author Page: www.amazon.com/author/davidbogart

Website: www.dbbooks.us

Email: dbogart2@stny.rr.com

Cover graphics designed by David V. Bogart, my son. Another great job! Thank you, David!

TABLE OF CONTENTS

CHAPTER ONE..1

    WHY DO WE STAY IN OUR HOMETOWN? 1

CHAPTER TWO...8

    THE BEGINNING ROOTS OF BINGHAMTON 8

CHAPTER THREE 24

    THE BINGHAMTON AREA IS BEAUTIFUL!...................24

CHAPTER FOUR 56

    THE ARCHITECTURE OF BINGHAMTON 56

CHAPTER FIVE 115

    CAROUSEL CAPITAL OF THE WORLD!.....................115

CHAPTER SIX...124

    BINGHAMTON PARKS AND MUSEUMS 124

CHAPTER SEVEN 203

    SPECIAL EVENTS IN BINGHAMTON.........................203

CHAPTER EIGHT 238

    SPECIALTY FOODS AND RESTAURANTS...................238

CHAPTER NINE 270

    BINGHAMTON SPORTS AND ENTERTAINMENT! 270

CHAPTER TEN 291

    TWO GREAT UNIVERSITIES IN BINGHAMTON....................291

CHAPTER ELEVEN 300

    TRADITIONS FROM OUR PAST CONTINUE........................300

PREFACE

I wrote the book based on what I have heard others say about the Binghamton area. Some things that I have seen on the internet gave me all the motivation needed. I gained the inspiration from bringing my family up in Binghamton, and I expressed that with everything here that surrounds us. I feel it is necessary to thank my parents for their decision to live here. They did not waiver on living in the area and thought it was an excellent place to raise a family. That idea trickled down to me as I stayed the course with my family that I love so much. I have always felt that the city takes a lot of unwarranted abuse. There has been no second-guessing on my part about living here.

There is so much information about Binghamton on the internet. The web was a great source of information to share. I believed photos would be a crucial part of the book. It was a challenge for sure to use anyone's work, so I grabbed my camera and circled the city many times to get the best pictures I could. I also must thank my friends and neighbors around me. I was always willing to help in a bad situation. They have still formed a closely knit feeling, a feeling of belonging. Neighbors show a love for the area and the need to keep this a safe place to raise our families. Some friends shared some local stories with you as well. I thank them very much.

CHAPTER ONE

WHY DO WE STAY IN OUR HOMETOWN?

"This was his hometown. And as his famous quote goes, Everybody has to have a hometown, Binghamton is mine," said Anne Serling, daughter of Rod Serling.

The first thing that I need to get off my chest is to say that there is no letter "p" in Binghamton's word. Whew, glad that is out of the way. I can remember as a child while growing up here in Binghamton and hearing about Rod Serling. I always admired his love for his hometown. I never met him, although it would have been an honor that I would have never forgotten. As I grew older, there were two things about Rod Serling that made a big impression. He accomplished the work with his craft and never forgot his roots of the time he had here as a young boy. He never spoke badly about Binghamton and displayed pride in his hometown. We have memories of Rod Serling all around our city to this day. It is a pleasure to stop by and see them with a smile that shares his devotion to the place where he grew up.

When I wrote this book, I must tell you I had many other requests concerning what I should include. Although our history here is quite impressive, I wanted to write about the subject of having that hometown feeling. Why do some people choose to leave their hometown and live elsewhere? Why do some people stay? Another question that I always had and still do. Why do some speak so severely about the place where they grew up? Is it that bad living here in Binghamton? I do not think so. Occasionally I read articles that someone wrote about Binghamton. Comments from a person who once lived here and moved away. Some of the descriptive phrases they use are earth-shattering. Binghamton is not New York City or Los Angeles, so do not expect it to be. However, it is a great city with an unbelievable past, and it is a great place to raise a family.

During my life, I have changed somewhat from being the type of person who always felt the need to be right to the person who tries to listen more. I keep my opinions to myself. However, after hearing others speak with so much negativity, I felt the need to express my thoughts on that subject. Some comments from others about Binghamton on the internet are amazing! Unbelievable words! I respect the right for others that choose to move. However, I do not see the need to degrade where you grew up, just as I do not need to write about other places.

There is no perfect place on this earth that does not have some issues. Binghamton is no exception anywhere else, so there is no need to criticize our hometown. I can assure those who remained here that your parents cared enough about us when we were children. They lived in a place they thought was safe. They felt the importance of finding an excellent place to raise a family. Some things or situations are worth standing up for. To make it a better place to live, I stayed in Binghamton.

The decision to write this book was a learning experience for me. I have learned that, mostly, others involved with the history of Binghamton stay very close to their work. I felt it would be an essential part of this book to take pictures of the city as it looks now rather than how it looked in the past. So, if you saw a maniac driving around the town snapping photos, that was me! In doing my research, I got information through public methods readily available online or from the library. I will write this book with my twist. I am a lifelong resident of the City of Binghamton and have lived here for 64 years. This book will contain my reasons for choosing Binghamton to be my home. The intent of this book is not to offend anyone who moved away.

Why do some people leave? I think there are many reasons. First, let us start with our children moving away from home to attend college. They gain the first glimpse of independence. It is a different feeling for them as they morph into a world explorer. Although explorers still need help from mom and dad, it is an exciting part of their life. However, it is a new world, and the exposure to new people in their lives creates a more comfortable feeling of living elsewhere. The new surroundings also provide them the chance to be free of the evil empire of parents and the option to make their own choices in life. Indeed, an understandable reason to leave the place where they grew up.

Others leave their hometown because their family went. They still desire to be close to family, so when the family moves, so do they. There are many reasons families leave here or anywhere for sure. It could be weather and the ultimate dream of living year-round in a warm climate. It takes a person to stay in an area that goes through the changes of seasons. I believe you need to have a love of watching the seasons change to stay here. The bottom line is you must live your life the way you wish. If the weather is a determining factor, then that is where you need to be. However, take it easy on those of us that love the seasons!

Some people move away because they get married. Here, we move for the love of our partner. That is an understandable reason to move. However, it is still important to remember your roots. Love is such a determining factor in a situation like that. There are many instances that either the husband or the wife will make that sacrifice. A move like that is not a bad thing and delivers the chance to have a close involvement in another family's hometown location.

Probably one of the most substantial reasons that some choose to move is employment. It is so difficult to get good jobs to make a living in some areas of our country. The answer for many is to move to where the money is with a goal of reliable employment. Besides, sometimes the type of job you study for in college is just not available in your hometown. That decision leaves us with a choice of either settling for something else than you went to school for or making a move to a new location. Many times, this could cause moving away to another city. Sometimes, it could even be in another country.

Other reasons include the belief that you cannot find that person to share your life within a specific location. I have always believed that maybe you just are not going to the right places in that regard. I have also heard, "there is nothing for me here!" Perhaps that is true, but have you tried all the options? In today's time, it is essential to think creatively. I still am a big believer in the old saying, "where there is a will, there is a way!" Also, I have heard things like, "there is nothing to do here. It is boring." All I can say is, read this book!

I also believe that there is a real stigma about those who choose to stay in the place where we grew up. Implications made about our lack of initiative or drive needed to be successful. I am certainly not in agreement with that. I feel that the value of friends and family that we grow up with outweighs the urge to move away. We have a more secure network living in the area where we grew up. That strength is more important than money or employment for many that stay. The cost of living is a precious measurement in the decision to move away. There are increasing amounts of jobs today that you can work from home with good pay. Also, for those willing, opportunities exist to start your home-based businesses. I know I started my business, and there are opportunities out there for others who are eager to do that.

I will say that the most important reason that I stayed here in my hometown of Binghamton would have to be my wife and family. My family is here, and I felt the need to keep close to my parents, specifically my mother, for many reasons I have discussed in a previous book. Also, I fell in love with my high school sweetheart, who was also from this area. Although my wife grew up in Johnson City, we lived in Binghamton. She never even mentioned once moving to a different place.

Living near your family can challenge you too, but in this life, the one thing you can always count on is the love of your family. My wife, Barbara, was the reason I stayed in Binghamton. I turned down opportunities to move to Rochester, Buffalo, and Albany in our marriage's early years. Children play an essential part in a decision to move too. You can see the reasons for leaving a specific area can be the same as staying. I am a firm believer that the grass is not always greener on the other side of the street. Do we have issues here in Binghamton? We sure do. Are there any locations that do not have their problems? I do not think so.

This book is not about history, although history is a part of why I remained here. The book is more about people, places, foods, and much more that played a significant role in my decision to stay in my hometown of Binghamton. I know Binghamton is not everyone's cup of tea, but to me, it is home sweet home! So, sit back, relax, and take a trip with me to the past, present, and future of Binghamton.

"For whatever else I may have had, or lost, or will find, I've still got a hometown. This, nobody's gonna take away from me." ~ Rod Serling.

This marker appears on the grounds of Binghamton High School. Rod Serling attended school here, while we knew the school was Binghamton Central.

CHAPTER TWO

THE BEGINNING ROOTS OF BINGHAMTON

Let us take a trip way back in time, back to a site at the Susquehanna and Chenango River junction. At this confluence, there was a village of Iroquois Native Americans with the name of Ochenang. If you look at the name of that village and put the "O" and the end of the word chenang, it becomes Chenango! An area that was rich in agriculture is part of the Binghamton area.

The Iroquois Native Americans inhabited the site here until shortly after the American Revolution. The calendar was in the year 1779. Soon after that time, a brigade of troops under General James Clinton began their journey to meet General Sullivan and establish a military camp. The two generals met and camped here for two nights. The Iroquois Confederacy comprised Oneida and Onondaga tribes and inhabited Binghamton's area as we know it. These tribes would be a threat to the revolutionists' efforts. So, the Sullivan-Clinton combined troops had the terrible task of removing the Native American population located here. The forces won a decisive victory in Newtown, which is now known as Elmira, N.Y.

Our history tells us it was difficult for people to travel around back. Binghamton opened its first weekly stage service in the year 1816. That service-connected us with Newburgh and Owego. Hard to imagine a stage service here, but this was the start of community travel from Binghamton!

William Bingham now enters the scene. William was a wealthy state leader and banker living in Philadelphia. He also served in the United States Senate and was the first speaker of the Philadelphia House of Representatives. William used his riches to become a significant land developer and became the owner of the area we live in today. He was also a broker involved with the Louisiana Purchase.

One of Bingham's agents, a settler named Judge Joshua Whitney Jr., named our town Binghamton. The name honored his employer, William Bingham, even though William, oddly enough, never set one foot in our area. Joshua also developed our very first street plan for Binghamton and found new ways to have people move into our site.

Then, in 1806, this area split from Tioga County and formed the new county of Broome. The name for Broome County came into existence after Lieutenant-Governor John Broome in his honor. Before that time, they knew merely our area as Chenango Point. Binghamton became incorporated as a village in 1834. Thirty-three years later, Binghamton became incorporated as a city. Our own Binghamton University recognizes William Bingham to this day with the naming of their Bingham Hall!

The area was growing, and methods of transportation were changing too. The Erie Canal had opened, and the other regions, including Binghamton, were eager to connect to the canal to aid in trade development. To do this, the Chenango Canal was born. The Chenango Canal was ninety-seven miles and joined Binghamton in Utica and Erie. The Chenango Canal finally reached Binghamton in 1837.

However, the addition of the Chenango Canal was short-lived. Methods used to move goods from one area to the next were happening so fast that the Canal's advantages could not match trains' arrival. In 1848, the first passenger train from Erie arrived at the station. The Binghamton area became the central transportation hub for travel. The appearance of trains changed the entire atmosphere for Binghamton. We were the place to go!

As time passed to the Civil War era, the Binghamton area saw some more significant changes. Daniel S. Dickinson was our local politician. He served in the United States Senate from 1844 to 1850 and helped to fulfill the needs of ammunitions and other war products. Daniel brought assembly-line factory work to Binghamton, realizing the market. The manufacturing of guns and many other products took place in our region.

The Industrial Revolution saw many new major industries opening Binghamton as well. Stow Manufacturing relied on the flexible shaft's invention (the shaft allowed the transition of power or rotary motion through a curved path). The lumber industry transformed into a large furniture and wagon business. The business was booming in Binghamton.

However, Binghamton changed with the first cigar manufacturing company around the year 1870. Within twenty years, over fifty factories were producing cigars here. The Binghamton area employed over five thousand people involved with cigars manufacturing and made over one hundred million cigars each year. Binghamton ranked second in the production of cigars, right behind New York City. People were now coming from many countries to Binghamton to work in the cigar industry. I feel this was the beginning of a real melting pot here in Binghamton. Many other companies produced over two hundred different products in Binghamton with employment opportunities. Binghamton was becoming the place to live!

During this time, the Binghamton area transformed with the growth of older architecture throughout the city. The business was excellent, and the people living here invested in buildings that reflected the beauty of that time's architecture. Particularly in the **Court Street Historic District**, downtown, including the Broome County Courthouse and the Binghamton City Hall and all the other buildings in and around Chenango Street.

Another area of Historical significance is the **Railroad Terminal District**. That district includes twenty buildings involved with the railroad, such an essential part of our development. Another historical area is the State Street-Henry Street Historic District, containing landmark buildings and dedication to the arts. Also, Binghamton has the Abel Tract Historic District, including over one thousand beautiful homes.

Beautiful mural pained in downtown Binghamton.

Also, we have many museums, and homes that proudly still show the architecture of that era. Late in the nineteenth century, Binghamton gained the nickname of the "**Parlor City**." Many residential homes sprang up, built from the wealth of business. Most of the houses all had a parlor where friends and family met while visiting. Hence, the nickname Parlor City was born.

Around 1854, Binghamton's second-largest employer was a shoe manufacturer, Lester Brother's Boot and Shoe Company. Their business became so strong that they had no room to grow. So, they picked up their stakes and, in 1890, moved to land west of the city of Binghamton. That move created their town called Lestershire, which is now known as Johnson City. That company continued to grow and later became known as Endicott Johnson Shoes. Their growth employed over twenty thousand workers and helped to create the villages of Johnson City and Endicott. Endicott Johnson developed combat boots that our troops used during both World Wars. However, I felt the most crucial thing that Endicott Johnson accomplished was how they treated their workers. They welcomed all immigrants to be employed there, including Italians, Germans, Poles, Czechs, Slovaks, Lithuanians, Russians, Ukrainians, and Greeks. They accepted all religions, including Roman Catholics, Eastern Orthodox Catholics, and Jews. These were all welcome to add to the mix of English, Scots, and Irish who were already working there.

Endicott Johnson arch dedicated by the workers.

That was not all; Endicott-Johnson created the phrase "Home of the Square Deal." That phrase is still visible today along Main Street as you enter Johnson City and Endicott. Two beautifully constructed arches stand there today as a constant reminder. Endicott Johnson workers formed these arches! The square deal created the eight-hour workday for their workers. The agreement also built affordable no-interest houses for workers to purchase. It also created libraries, theaters, schools, parks, race tracks, hospitals, and fire stations.

The George F. Johnson (commonly known and addressed as "George F.") family donated area parks and six carousels to the triple city area. Thus, it created the area's second nickname as the "Carousel Capital of the United States." The donation of the parks and carousels came with one condition from George F. Johnson. The admission to ride the carousels is forever free and is open from Memorial Day to Labor Day. He felt carousels contributed to a happy life and would help youngsters grow into durable and useful citizens. Today, EJ Footwear, LLC, operates as a unit of the Ohio-based Rocky Shoes and Boots Inc. Endicott Johnson was a company that genuinely cared for its workers and showed it.

He wanted all the carousels manufactured by the Allan Herschell Companies of North Tonawanda, N.Y. He is insisting on using the country fair style while adding calliope sounds. Today, you can still hear the Wurlitzer Band Organs play in Recreation Park and Ross Park. Broome County has the only carousel collection in the world. Less than one hundred seventy antique carousels are remaining in the United States and Canada, and six are located right here in the Triple Cities area.

All six are now on the New York State Historic Register and the National Register of Historic Places. Binghamton is home to a carousel exhibit and gift shop. They are both in the Ross Park carousel area. The display shows the history of the carousels and George F. Johnson's role in developing them. George F. Johnson cared about people and strangely affected my desire to live here. During this time, Binghamton's population grew substantial, now doubling every ten to fifteen years.

Simultaneously, Johnson City (formerly Lestershire) and Endicott's planned community (incorporated in 1906) were growing. Another strong business that started in Binghamton in 1889 was the **Bundy Manufacturing Company.** Harlow Bundy organized the Bundy Time Recording Company in Binghamton. His business was successful in attracting many new investors. Before long, his time recorders appeared throughout the world. After merging with other companies, the International Time Recording and Tabulating Company outgrew its Binghamton roots and moved to Endicott, N.Y. In 1914. Thomas Watson, Sr. used his corporate leadership and moved the company into a new era. The company's success resulted in changing the name of the company to International Business Machines. IBM in 1924. IBM became a computer company that now employs over one-quarter million workers worldwide.

In 1878, another large business formed in Binghamton. Jonas Kilmer invented the patent medicine Swamp-Root Elixir. He became wealthy from this product and built the Kilmer building. **The Kilmer building** is where he manufactured the goods that the company distributed all over the United States. A beautiful piece of architecture, the building is still standing today.

HOME IS WHERE MY HEART IS

The Kilmer family also had a beautiful mansion in which he lived on Riverside Drive. His son Willis Sharpe Kilmer owned and managed the Binghamton Press newspaper and became involved with several downtown buildings. Also, he served as a bank president and as a leader in various social organizations. His hobbies also included owning horses. He held "Exterminator," the winner of the 1918 Kentucky Derby.

In 1907, the Alanzo Roberson house became a new part of the **Roberson Center for the Arts and Sciences**. The house is in the Italian Renaissance style and is still standing today. A turn-of-the-century businessperson would love the beautiful style of this home.

Another big business in the area was the Anthony & Scovill Company. The Ansco Company began in 1907 and manufactured paper, film, and cameras in our city. However, in 1940, the company changed into the Agfa-Ansco Company.

The new company now was the second-largest manufacturer of photographic supplies. During World War II, the U.S. government became suspicious of its German partners. As a result, the government seized control of the company during the war. The company was never quite the same after that. Ansco eventually became the paper and film division of GAF Corporation. Anitec Division of International Paper formed from its film manufacturing plant.

We now approach the year 1910 and the birth of The Binghamton Street Railway. This railway, along with other electric trolleys, is now transporting our local citizens throughout Broome County. One accessible location was the Ross Park Zoo! Our Ross Park Zoo is within the top five oldest zoos in the United States! I must admit that a part of me would have loved to ride our trolley cars.

During the height of the Great Depression, Edwin A. Link of Binghamton completed his dream to develop the pilot trainer, otherwise known as a flight simulator. In 1928, Edwin A. Link built his first flight trainer in the basement of his father's player piano and organ factory where he was working. His visions through Link Aviation using their many forms have led the world in the training of pilots.

During World War II. Edwin Link's "Blue Box" trainers became essential to our role in the war. The Blue Box trained thousands of allied pilots to win decisive battles of Britain, Europe, and the Pacific. The technology he created has developed into a virtual reality world of products we still use today. Edwin Link developed the idea of a training simulation to include driving simulators, helicopters, naval, and NASA rocket simulators. His dreams are now part of the Singer Corporation. Singer makes Link trainers for the military, commercial pilots, and astronauts.

HOME IS WHERE MY HEART IS

The Binghamton area had many companies that were involved with the growth of the defense business. Large companies such as IBM, General Electric, Universal, Link and relied heavily on the defense segment's income. As time went on, the defense business floundered. Binghamton became a part of a downward economic trend. Many of the people that moved here felt that the opportunities they dreamed of were no longer achievable. The population in our area declined.

Binghamton had a lackluster effort to rebound during the era of the 1960s. Large empty lots and empty storefronts now seemed to be the norm. Binghamton has now taken on a significant role in providing housing to college students, mainly from Binghamton University. Also, Binghamton is making strides in the Healthcare and Medical fields, providing a surge to get our area back to where it once was. Binghamton also has an added interest in supporting small business growth to stimulate future growth for the city.

Despite our rich business history, Binghamton has always been the story of our people. All the immigrants and their different ethnic food, costume, languages, "Gold Dome" churches, and heritage, have made the Binghamton area a real melting pot. The legacy of our businesses, such as Endicott Johnson and our continual ethnic and business origin, makes this region a healthy and vibrant part of American Culture.

I felt it would be an exciting addition to the book by adding some personal stories from our area. Some friends of mine stepped forward to share some experiences and stories from their past. A good friend of mine, Debbie, had some thoughts about the good ole days. I was so happy she agreed to share the following story with us all.

Remembering the Good Ole Days!

Years ago, there used to be a movie theater in Binghamton on 60 Exchange Street. The following story is from Debbie Petrosky, who used to be a regular customer of the Capitol Theater.

The Capitol Theater, Photo courtesy of Dave Boann

She tells us a story about her uncle, who was the Capital theater manager back in the day. They well knew this theater for vaudeville acts besides being a movie theater. Her aunt and uncle got to know many movie stars that would come to the theater to act in vaudeville shows or attend events when their new movies opened. Although she does not have a memory of all the famous entertainers they met, she remembers quite a few of them. She offered her aunt and uncle to meet many of the stars. They became so close to some of them that many of the stars would send them Christmas cards every year. Danny Kay was one that they met and became good friends. Can you just imagine yourself going back in time to a more carefree existence?

She can clearly remember the first time she went to the movie theater. She went for the first and only time her entire family got together to see the same movie. She had a great family outing as they went to see the film "The Ten Commandments." You could see a motion picture for only twenty-five cents. She can remember getting a soda and popcorn for an additional fifty-cents. Those were the days!

In 1966, Binghamton's city demolished the Capitol Theater landmark to make room for a Binghamton Savings Bank parking lot. However, her uncle landed on his feet. Using his experience as the Capital theater manager, he quickly got the job to manage the Strand and Riviera Movie Theater complex.

With her uncle managing, she benefitted by going to see movies with her friends for free. That made them happy because it gave them more money to spend on popcorn, soda, and candy. It still amazed her at how little things cost back then. She can also remember thinking it was a lot of money. It is costly to go to the movies today— quite a change.

Debbie remembers going with her friends to see the film "Texas Chain Saw Massacre." Back that movie was as scary as you could get. As they exited the theater, the sky was getting dark as the evening set in. Wanting to get home as quickly as possible, they crossed over the State Street Bridge. It was wintertime with snow on the ground. You can just guess what they would do next. Of course, kids would throw snow; that is what we do!

The beautiful architecture of the Strand movie theater is still standing.

As they crossed the bridge, a group threw some snow over the bridge into the river. The snow was flying all around as they laughed and played. You will never guess what happened next. Debbie went to throw snow over the bridge and think what she threw instead? The snow stayed in one hand, and she threw her coin purse over the railing instead. She was so happy to be going home with $1.50 in her coin purse. Back then, a lot of money for someone her age. She watched in absolute horror as her coin purse went kerplunk into the river water. There went her $1.50 sinking in the ripples of the splash in the river.

So, if you find a coin purse as you ramble along the river banks or snag it while fishing, call me. I will make sure it gets back to the proper owner!

Thanks for sharing your story, Debbie Petrosky.

CHAPTER THREE

THE BINGHAMTON AREA IS BEAUTIFUL!

Nature abounds surrounding the Binghamton area. Visions of rolling hills and forest-type landscapes encompass the borders of our city. Nature's beauty becomes more enhanced with the picturesque waterways flowing from the Susquehanna, Chenango, Tioughnioga, and Otselic rivers. Binghamton lies in the Allegheny Plateau section of the northern Appalachian Plateau. I have always considered our area here to be exquisite.

About twenty thousand years ago, a thick ice sheet (estimated at 3,000 feet) completely covered our area. As that glacier melted, it formed and uncovered the Allegheny and Appalachian Mountains. Besides cutting the mountains, the glacier cut the Plateau into this beautiful hilly area. The streams that were born during this time eroded the sedimentary rock here, which helped to develop our beautiful hills and mountains.

The melting glaciers also deposited loose materials that formed outwash plains. These plains served as a groundwater source and provided fertile soil for farming and an excellent solid base for building buildings. The soil base comprises Chemung rock, sandstone, and shale formed by delta deposits and is a large part of Binghamton's bottom.

The Susquehanna River flows one hundred miles to the north to Otsego Lake in Cooperstown, N.Y. The Susquehanna River is the longest river on the East Coast of the United States, and including its watershed, it is the sixteenth largest river in the United States. Near the South Washington Street Bridge, the Chenango River becomes a confluence with the Susquehanna River. From that intersection point, the Susquehanna River continues for four hundred and forty-four total miles. The river continues to the west along New York's southern tier and eventually turns southeast through central Pennsylvania. Perhaps a little-known fact is that the Susquehanna River drains over nineteen million gallons of fresh water into the Chesapeake Bay every minute!

Curiosity got the best of me about the meaning of the word "Susquehanna." After some research, I found that the name's history came from the Delaware Indian term, *"Sisa'we'hak'hanna,* which means Oyster River." Huge oyster beds were at the mouth of the river and farmed by the Native Americans. In Pennsylvania, the Delaware Indian Nations lived in twenty villages along the river.

The Chenango River, which joins the Susquehanna River in Binghamton, is about ninety miles long. In the early days of the city, the Chenango River was an important part. The Chenango Canal was a crucial link from the river, which made a connection possible to the Erie Canal that aided our trade area. Workers in our site built the canal by hand and hard labor. In the Binghamton area and beyond, you will see markers for the Chenango Canal as a tribute to its existence. Binghamton eventually abandoned the Chenango Canal project and progressed with the popularity of the railroad. The word Chenango translates from the Oneida tribe with the meaning of "bull thistle."

There is a beautiful parcel of land next to the Washington Street bridge where the Chenango River and the Susquehanna River meet. A picturesque piece of land called Confluence Park. The city has maintained the beauty of the area with continuous first-rate landscaping. Connected with the park is a paved trail along the Chenango River we call the River Walk. The trail is about a mile and a half and will bring you to Cheri Lindsey Memorial Park on the north side of the city. You can take a stroll on the River Walk or go for a bicycle ride.

Confluence Park is a wonderful place to have a quiet seat while looking out at the motion of the rivers. It is also a place where you can fish and is a favorite spot for photography. Confluence Park is a local favorite for prom and wedding pictures too.

Confluence marker acknowledging the Sullivan Expedition.

Archaeological investigations, most completed by local universities over the past 50 or more years, identified traces of past Native American camps and villages that once dotted the banks of these two rivers, particularly near the confluence area.

There is a historical significance to this spot as well. Over two hundred and thirty-six years ago. Continental Army General James Clinton's troops reached the confluence of the Susquehanna and Chenango Rivers to join the Sullivan Expedition. The spot is displaying a monument marking a historical moment of the Revolutionary War. Over a thousand troops, horses and supplies were all on board the boats as they arrived.

The 1779 Sullivan Expedition formed as ordered by George Washington and conducted by the Continental Army, during the American Revolutionary War against Loyalists and the four Nations of the Iroquois which had sided with the British. The Americans carried out the campaign as a response to attacks by the British-allied Iroquois in 1778.

Confluence Park as viewed from a distance.

There are beautiful scenes from the park.

There are wonderful scenes in the park.

There are great scenes in the park.

There are beautiful scenes from the park.

There are wonderful scenes in the park.

There are great scenes in the park.

Scenes from the park.

There are beautiful scenes from the park.

There are wonderful scenes in the park.

There are wonderful scenes in the park.

This photo is a beautiful scene from the Chenango River.

This photo is a unique view of the Susquehanna River from one of Binghamton's many
bridges.

I have always thought that sunset pictures are beautiful. These two pictures just give you that laid-back, lazy feeling of summer.

Chenango River

Sometimes we do not take the time to sit back, relax, and enjoy the beauty of the nature that surrounds us. I have always been so delighted at how nature surrounds us in Binghamton. The rivers are beautiful and are a big reason for the history we have here. I have always enjoyed looking around our area to see the hills that surround us. It is a welcome alternative to having flat land as far as the eye can see.

Susquehanna River

Above: Cheri Lindsey Park views, below: Confluence Park.

Beautiful views of Chenango River from Cheri Lindsey Park

Otsiningo Park is below.

Downtown Binghamton, below: Looking down in the city from State Hospital Hill

Chenango River View, below: The Skirmisher Statue in Confluence Park.

The Skirmisher

It is not only the beauty of nature that I enjoy so much here; we have some beautiful public art throughout the city. Here are some examples that I would like to share. I am amazed that every time I drive around the city it seems like I discover another example.

There is a great interest in the arts in Binghamton. Broome County had taken an active interest in promoting public art. Public art can take many shapes, forms, and sizes, but it is in places that everyone can view and enjoy. We can enjoy dozens of creative art installations throughout Binghamton in our downtowns, neighborhoods, parks, schools, and even businesses.

Beau Stanton, an internationally known artist, painted this mural in Binghamton. The colors of the leaves in the fall inspired him and the patinated copper color of the courthouse dome. The ribbons follow the two rivers that define Binghamton. This beautiful painting is a showcase outside the Garage Taco Bar, a well-known restaurant in downtown Binghamton.

Lady Liberty Beau Stanton, Paint on brick, 2018.

Beautiful Public Art even decorates businesses.

My favorite, Parlor City.

CHAPTER FOUR

THE ARCHITECTURE OF BINGHAMTON

As a young boy growing up, it always amazed me at the intricate designs of buildings and homes all around the city. I am not foolish enough to think that Binghamton is the only city that has excellent architecture. However, I will say that the architecture's beauty instilled within me a feeling of being home. I can only describe that feeling by saying that it created a deep love for this city from the knowledge of what others did here before my time.

INEBRIATE ASYLUM, BINGHAMTON.

The Binghamton Inebriate Asylum

Let us start with the Binghamton Inebriate Asylum. Now this location has always fascinated me. Even as a young boy, it seemed like a scary place to me. Maybe that look of the gothic revival design made me feel that way. It reminded me of a site directly out of a Batman movie like Gotham City. However, the architecture was magnificent! A classic piece of architecture that still stands long after the year 1864. I initially knew the building as the Binghamton Inebriate Asylum and was the first building to treat alcoholism as a mental disorder. Looking back now, it amazed me we still had significant issues with drugs and alcohol that far back in time.

The Gothic Revival exterior, designed by the well-known and famous architect Isaac G. Perry was a perfect choice. The asylum converted to a mental institution back in the year 1879 and continued in that capacity until 1993, when it officially closed. During that time, the building became known as Binghamton State Hospital. In the year of 1997, the building became a Registered National Historic Landmark. In 2015, Binghamton University took stewardship of the building and will proceed with the rehabilitation of the building. I look f to the future when perhaps there will be an onsite museum for all to enjoy.

The hospital was the first significant project of Isaac G. Perry, and he was the first official architect for the state of New York. His work became so well known that in 1883, Governor Grover Cleveland appointed him to take charge of the State capital's construction. Before he retired in 1899, he had quite a list of accomplished architectural structures.

Other buildings that Isaac designed in the Binghamton area include The Phelps Mansion, Monday Afternoon Club, General Edward F. Jones House (21 room Queen Anne Victorian mansion), and the J. Start Wells House. The total number of projects completed on the National Register of Historic Places is too many to list.

It is so refreshing when doing a project that you believe in when you meet good people. I wanted to thank A. D. Wheeler for giving his permission to use these memorable photographs that he took, capturing the inside in the Binghamton Inebriate Asylum.

Binghamton State Hospital

I think the words that he wrote in an email to me say it all. "So many of these hospitals were beautiful for all the wrong reasons. One of the other reasons I do what I do is that I would like these places to be re-purposed and used for good. Not to forget those who suffered there, but to honor them and bring new happy light to these sad monuments of lousy humanity. Sadly, most of them become wrapped up in political red tape, as is most of our world today. I will keep fighting the good fight, though, as I know you will as well." We cannot forget what others went through before us. I genuinely believe that. Whenever I go up to that "Castle on the Hill," I wonder how the patients must have felt back then looking out the windows. Please visit his website www.theexplorographer.com.

Binghamton State Hospital, beautiful ornate hallway.

Binghamton State Hospital, beautiful ornate hallway, patient rooms

Please enjoy these captured moments from the inside of the Binghamton Inebriate Asylum. Below, they knew the eye in the chapel's ceiling to patients as God looking down on them!

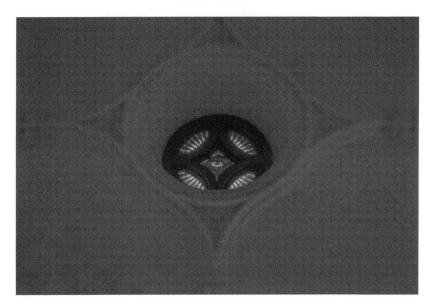

HOME IS WHERE MY HEART IS

The intricate and beautiful woodwork that surrounded the hallways, windows, and doors there! Let us remember the courage of those who suffered there.

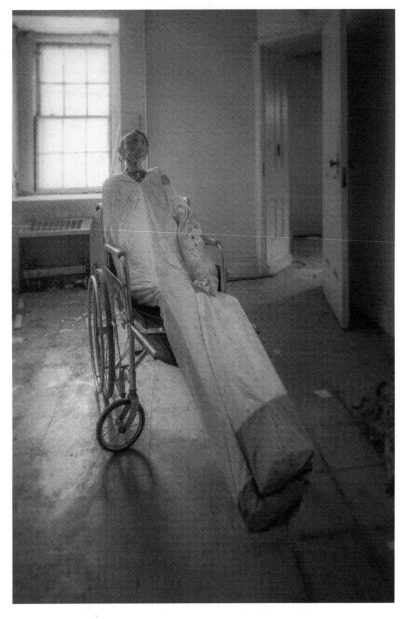

The figure is not a patient, just an example of a room.

Another place in the facility. I can only imagine those who looked out these windows long ago. The photo below contains one of the beautifully decorated stairways that exist in this marvelous piece of architecture.

These photos are examples of the intricately designed halls and stairways.

I spoke with a couple of friends about the stories they have witnessed at this location. I hope you enjoy the following two stories. The stories are from someone who worked in the facility for many years.

The Woman in the White Dress

It was just another night at the Castle on the Hill, on the east side of Binghamton. The Binghamton Health Center has its security force on site. The original building is still vacant, replaced by a modern facility on the same grounds. Even though many buildings remain empty now, it is essential to maintain scheduled visits to each location for security.

On this night, a security officer had just checked in to begin his shift. The officer stopped to talk with his co-workers to see if there were any specific directions for the night. There was nothing new to report, so he got into his patrol car and left their office to start his rounds just as he usually did. He drove around the facility, stopping at each building checkpoint to ensure security. Everything seemed to be the same as any other night. He proceeded to his last stop and got out of his car to check the building's safety. Everything was secure, so he climbed back into his car and headed back to the security office.

During his drive back to the office, he had to pass the old wooden gazebo area. As he approached the site of the pavilion, he noticed something moving in that grassy area. Now, getting a little anxious, he stopped his car. He opened the car door, stood up, and looked with some concern around the gazebo. He saw what looked like a woman traveling through the grass. She was wearing a long white dress. It was dark, very early in the morning hours, so he was a bit confused about how or why anyone would be out in this area, especially a woman! He wanted to be sure he saw correctly, so he shined his flashlight towards her and shouted, "are you ok?" There was no answer. He asked again, no response. At that moment, he noticed something about her he could not explain or believe. His anxiety level was high, and he immediately got back into his car as he drove back to the security office as quickly as possible.

Binghamton State Hospital, Gazebo!

He entered the security office and proceeded to the back room, looking straight ahead. He walked right past his fellow security guards without saying so much as one word. He dashed to the farthest place in the office and just sat there in silence.

His fellow security guards knew something was wrong, but did not know what it could be. So, they left him alone for a bit of time. After a short while, his fellow officers came into the room to see what was wrong. They entered the back room to notice their friend sitting quietly there. His face was as white and pale as a ghost!

They asked him, "What is wrong? Your face is as white as a ghost!"

He answered, "on my way back to the office. I saw a woman wearing a white dress going towards the gazebo."

They looked at him and laughed. "What's the big deal with that?"

He replied, "She wasn't walking. She was floating along the top of the grass. No feet were touching the grass!!"

His fellow officers did not know what to say. They could see that he was very anxious about the whole situation. However, stories like this happened around the Castle on the Hill. His friends filled in for him that night and made the security rounds.

<u>Looking for a Solitaire Partner?</u>

The Binghamton Inebriate Asylum and the surrounding buildings are not without a history of spooky stories. I enjoyed visiting with a former employee who shared her memory of an event not that long ago. It was just another ordinary day of work for her. She worked in the Garvin building. As her workday progressed, she received a phone call from a fellow employee who worked on the building's third floor.

He said, "Hey, I need to show you something, but you need to come up here right away before it's too late! You will never believe this!"

With curiosity getting the best of her, she asked, "Why? What's the big secret?"

She explained she was working with another nurse.

He replied, "That's great. Both of you can come! I cannot tell you; I must show you. Hurry!"

The two women began their trip to see what the big commotion was all about. He worked on the third floor, so they had to go up two stories to the office in the Garvin building wing where they worked. They arrived in his office as quickly as they could, with great anticipation. After looking around to see nothing out of the normal, she asked,

"Is this a joke? I see nothing here?"

He answered, "What I wanted to show you is not here. Come over here by this window!"

They all moved over to the window together, looking across towards the other wing of the building. Mary's friend asked them to look down two floors within that specific wing. While they watched, he motioned for them to look at one window.

He asked, "What do you see?"

They replied, "A man is sitting at the table playing solitaire. What's so special about that?"

He replied, "There is no one there!"

They replied to him, "There sure is. I can see him sitting there playing solitaire!"

With that, her co-worker said, "Okay, I want you both to stay right where you are. Do not move! Just keep your eyes focused on that window. I'm going to go down there so I can prove it to you!"

Off he went. He had to go down two floors to enter that room, which was in a different wing. The two workers just stared at each other, and the window was trying hard not to laugh. Finally, they noticed him waving his arms over his head in the window. They could also see that just behind him and to his right was the gentleman. He was still sitting at the table playing cards.

What they saw next, they could not believe it! Her co-worker went over to the table where the man was playing cards and started waving his arms through the air where the man sat. His arms and hands went through this man. Both women continued to see the man still enjoying his card game. They were both silent and just stared at this man playing cards while they waited for him to come back to his office.

He said, "I just had to share this with someone. It does not happen often, and I find it so difficult to prove it when it does. I'm so glad you could see him, so others don't think I'm crazy," So if you are looking for a solitaire partner, check the windows at the building on the hill. He still could roam the grounds and looking for a partner.

Thanks for sharing your stories with us, Mary Nichols Adams

Getting back to the beautiful architecture here in Binghamton. I am proud to share another historical landmark, the Broome County Courthouse.

The courthouse is a colossal structure rising two and one-half stories high. The architects built the courthouse on a raised foundation shaped as a Latin Cross. Sitting on top of the Courthouse is an elegant copper dome that contains eight clocks and includes a beautiful statue on the top. The building's initial construction was in 1897 and was in the shape of a "T." they added another south wing in 1917 to form the cross's shape.

This building was another fantastic project designed by New York State architect Isaac G. Perry. The courthouse is in the heart of the Court Street Historic District in Binghamton and became listed on the National Register of Historic Places in 1973. Isaac G Perry also designed the staircase within the building known as the "Million Dollar Staircase!"

Downtown Binghamton is the home of our beautiful Broome County Courthouse.

They built the original courthouse built in 1856 but they lost the building to fire in 1896. However, our newer courthouse made use of part of that initial foundation. I still marvel at the sight of the dome that tops our Broome County Courthouse.

I cannot believe that the first public hanging in Broome County history occurred on the Broome County Courthouse grounds back in 1871. Edward H. Rulloff was the first person with that distinction. Hard to imagine we had crowds of over five thousand people that gathered to watch that event. People came to witness the hanging from miles away. They even arrived on trains, and some attended the event from rooftops in downtown Binghamton. As you walk downtown now, it seems like something like that would have never taken place here, but it did.

While we are still in the beautiful downtown area, let us talk about the stunning architecture represented by several other buildings

in the Court Street Historic District. In 1984, the district became part
of the National Register of Historic Places.

Binghamton Courthouse Memorial Statues.

The **Court Street Historic District** includes one hundred and four different buildings in downtown Binghamton's heart. Many of the buildings went up long ago, as far back as the year 1840! The district comprises The Perry Building (also known as the Hills, McLean, and Haskins Department store), The Kilmer Press Building, First National Bank Building, The Security Mutual Life Building, and the old Binghamton Public Library Building. The Broome County Courthouse and the Binghamton City Hall are on the outer boundaries of the district.

This highly ornate four-story cast-iron building is one of Binghamton's unique and distinctive structures. Designed in 1876 by Isaac Perry in the middle of the Downtown Historic District on the corner of Court and Chenango Streets. Known as the **Perry Block**, the building is the only example of this type of architecture in the area. Notice the large windows and ornate architectural features typical of this form of construction.

The Perry Block building

One of New York's most famous architects, Isaac Gale Perry designed the Perry Block. Perry first came to Binghamton from New York City in 1858 to supervise construction of his first major architectural project, the New York State Inebriate Asylum.

With his wife Lucretia, Perry lived on the fourth floor of this building while operating his business on the floor below. A variety of businesses occupied the first and second floors, and residents will remember shopping here when it was home to McLean's, one of Binghamton's most popular department stores.

Throughout his career, Perry designed several structures in town, including the county courthouse across the street. In addition, he designed approximately 40 armories throughout the state, and completed the State Capitol in Albany. With all his accomplishments, some have described the Perry Block building as Perry's greatest structure.

It is interesting to note that this building played a starring role in the Hollywood movie "Liebestraum," filmed in Binghamton in 1991. The movie features several of Binghamton's historic buildings.

Press Building

The architectural design continued to the Binghamton **Press Building**. This building sprang up in 1904 and was to be the home of the Binghamton Press newspaper. Willis Sharp Kilmer was the owner and was insistent that this building would become the tallest building in Binghamton. That was a title that the building held until the State building came along in 1972. The Press Building was another example of Beaux arts architecture that we have here during this period.

Initially, the printing press in the building took up much of the basement and the first-floor space. The building entrance on the first floor was situated to watch the printing presses as they were functioning to make the newspaper. There were glass walls so people could attend. It was common to see crowds gather around outside towards printing times. The presses were in full view of the sidewalk. Sometimes, stores would stay open later in the evenings to take advantage of the crowds that would gather there. Mr. Kilmer was a shrewd businessperson and wanted to be the only newspaper in town. He would not let the Sun-Bulletin get in his way.

The **First National Bank** is another Historic landmark in Binghamton. The building has a unique flat iron shape and anchors the Court Street Historic District on Chenango and Court Street on the corner. The bank is across the street from The Perry Building and the Broome County Courthouse. Built-in the year 1929, it also became the headquarters for Crowley Foods in later years. However, during their life as the bank, they issued twenty-three different national currencies.

The First National Bank Building is a cornerstone in historic downtown Binghamton.

Now here is a building that I spent many Saturdays when I was the proud owner of a library card. The old **Binghamton Public Library** went up in 1903 with Isaac G. Perry as a consulting architect. Andrew Carnegie made a seventy-five-thousand-dollar donation to support the library. However, as time went on, space became more limited and eventually got to the point of disrepair. I remember the pride of marching up to the desk and getting each book stamped before I left. A new library opened in the year 2000.

Right next door to the old Public Library is another building that takes part in the Court Street Historic District.

The old Binghamton Public Library.

In 1904, the Security Mutual Life Building went up. The building would be the new site for the company's headquarters. It is a ten-story building built with the Beaux arts design.

The building contains a three-tiered facade, the bottom three floors with a very rusticated look, followed by five stories of brick and topped off with two stories made up using a very ornate design.

The door on the building resembles a stone bridge depicted on the company emblem. Today, it is a common sight in the evenings to see a wide variety of colored lights engulf the top two floors of this building. It is a beautiful sight during the holidays.

Security Mutual Building.

The last building in downtown Binghamton I always enjoyed seeing is the old **Binghamton City Hall**. Ingle & Almirall designed the building in the year 1897 in the Second Empire style.

Binghamton City Hall, now the Grand Royale Hotel

The building also features a mansard roof with a highly decorative cupola. Raymond Francis Almirall of Ingle and Almirall,

New York City, designed our City Hall. After graduation from Cornell University in 1891, he studied architecture under Victor Laloux at the Ecole des Beaux-Arts in Paris. He entered and won the design competition for the Binghamton City Hall project in 1896.

The old Binghamton City Hall is within the Court Street Historic District, listed in the National Register of Historic Places in 1971. In 1972, the city moved the City Hall to a new location, and after a ten-year vacancy, the building then turned into The Hotel Deville. The building remained a hotel, eventually changing to the name of The Grand Royale. The building recently closed as the building needs some improvements. I always paid attention to the two lions in front. They have a few rooms (55) available as I write today.

The latest update is the building is up and running again. The historic Grand Royale Hotel in downtown Binghamton has opened its doors again. The new owners have removed the entire second floor of the 118-year-old building and installed a new hookah lounge.

The old Binghamton City Hall is not without some mysterious events. After the City Hall moved to a new location, new owners renovated the building, and the site became the Hotel Deville. This hotel was exquisite as you could imagine and was the choice by most entertainers as the place to stay while performing at the Broome County Arena in downtown Binghamton.

The second-floor conference room was in use when City Hall occupied the building. The room included pictures of all the former mayors of Binghamton. That room became a dining area in the new hotel. Many times, for no reason, someone would walk through the room and appeared tripped. Not mean, but more like playfully. One day this happened to Sharon as she walked through the room. She stumbled, and for whatever reason, she looked towards the pictures and swore she saw one mayor in a photo. Wink at her!

She laughed and just knew he was the one responsible for the playful tripping that went on. It was my understanding that was something that always happened in that room.

Thank you, Sharon Joy Shadduck, for sharing your experience with us.

The Courthouse Tower Clock

Christ Church is a historic Episcopal Church In our city. It is a one-story bluestone structure with Gothic Revival elements. The church has a rectangular central section, housing the nave and aisles, an apse and bell tower on the east facade. The church has side entrances through transepts on the north and south elevations. Construction took place between 1853 and 1855, and Richard Upjohn, a well-known church architect designed the church. The Church became listed in the National Register of Historical places in 1974.

Trinity Memorial Church

Another example of fine architecture in our city is the historical Trinity Memorial Episcopal Church. Constructed in 1897 and is a High Victorian Gothic style structure constructed of bluestone with limestone water-table and trim. The front facade features a large square projecting tower with a side entrance and a smaller, secondary apse. Also on the front facade is a large Gothic arched window with geometric tracery and stained glass. In 1998, the church became listed on the National Register of Historical Places.

The **Railroad Terminal Historic District** comprises nineteen different buildings. I loved to visit the district when I was a young boy. I have to admit it still creates that same feeling inside me even to this day.

Delaware, Lackawanna and Western Railroad Station.

The buildings in this district were all built between the years 1876 and 1910. The facilities include warehouses, retail establishments, office buildings, and buildings that dealt with the trains' passengers. In 1986, the site became listed in the National Register of Historic Places. My dad used to work as an electrician for the railroad. His work area was located under the viaduct in a small building right next to the train station. I can remember times when we went into the station for lunch.

Binghamton Railroad District Railyard

Another little-known fact about Binghamton was the role that it played in the development of wireless communication. Specifically, the connection between the railroad station terminal and a moving train. The **Marconi Tower** still stands today. We were groundbreaking here in Binghamton with this type of communication.

Marconi Tower

© 2019 Kimberly Bogart

Marconi Tower Landmark Sign.

Next to the train station stands the Marconi Tower. The Marconi Tower transmitted messages to trains traveling between Binghamton and Scranton in Morse Code and became the world's first test for this communication type. The date was November 21, 1913, and although the first official announcement would be a week later, who would imagine such a great thing happening right here in my hometown?

Guglielmo Marconi invented the practical method of communicating with wireless telegraphy. He described it as merely using Morse Code and transmitting that through the wire to the antenna. The signal then traveled through space at the speed of light to the location intended. He invented that system in 1895, and by 1913, the Marconi wireless systems successfully worked in a variety of methods, including ship to shore communications. This method became one of the most effectively used for ship-to-shore communications. It was only one year before the Binghamton experiment that a Marconi system transmitted the critical message "SOS... Titanic Sinking, Please Rush All Possible help, Rush, Rush."

One of the most interesting pioneers in the history of Binghamton was Dr. S. Andral Kilmer. A Cornell University graduate, he was best known for marketing his uncle's Swamp Root patent medicine to where it became a household name. He developed the Swamp Root formula and started selling it in 1878.

As time went on, his brother Jonas helped the business. It was growing so fast it became difficult for Dr. Kilmer to run by himself. In fact, in 1892, Jonas bought out the business and added his son to help market and advertising. Swamp Root sales were through the roof, so to manage the business properly they built it as a place to manage and manufacture the product.

The Kilmer Building

The Kilmer building went up to handle the business, a beautiful six-story building placed right next to the railroad on the corner of Lewis and Chenango Streets. Downtown Binghamton became their headquarters in 1903.

However, in 1906 the government formed the Pure Food and Drug Act, which imposed regulations on the testing and labeling on patent medicines that made certain claims to our health. Their Swamp Root product became noted as fraud and advertised under false pretenses. The basis of the complaints centered on the lack of proof that Swamp Root could cure kidney or liver disease.

Dr. Kilmer's famous Swamp Root.

Kilmer mansion and Concord Temple.

Realizing that the Swamp Root business was in decline, Dr. Kilmer became heavily involved in Real Estate. Jonas M. Kilmer

House, also known as the Temple Concord, built in 1898 and is a large 3 1/2-story residence using an eclectic Victorian-era vocabulary. They primarily constructed it of stone and features irregular form and massing. The building shows character a variety of different sized gables and turrets, all surmounted by a high hipped roof clad in asbestos shingles. They listed it on the National Register of Historic Places in 2006.

Dr. Kilmer also had an interest in becoming involved in the newspaper business. Staying in the downtown area of our city, he formed the long running newspaper, The Binghamton Press. The Press building is twelve stories high, with beautiful architectural styles. The Press & Sun-Bulletin is still in circulation today. Some people rumored that Dr. Kilmer wanted to own the tallest building in the city. He built several other buildings in downtown Binghamton and three racing stables and estates.

The Sun Briar Court Stable in Binghamton was a massive piece of land totally dedicated to the breeding and care of race horses. We now know that section of land as Lourdes Hospital. Kilmer was the breeder of Raleigh Count, the winner of the 1928 Kentucky Derby. He was also the owner of Exterminator. Exterminator was the winner of the 1918 Kentucky Derby as named the American Horse of the Year in 1922. Dr. Kilmer was the breeder and owner of Sun Briar who was the largest money maker until Seabiscuit came onto the scene in 1939. They have elected Exterminator and Sun Briar to the

National Museum of Racing and Hall of Fame. Dr. Kilmer had both horses buried here locally.

The Kilmer Building

The diversity of this man fascinates me. Dr. Kilmer also owned a private yacht named Remlik (the name being Kilmer spelled backwards). The Navy purchased his yacht for to use World War I.

The Navy converted his yacht into an armed patrol vessel and renamed it the USS Remlik (SP-157).

Kilmer died in 1940, having amassed a fortune of some fifteen million, mostly from the sale of Swamp Root tonic, which is still for sale today.

Back in the day, as you stepped off the train, the Kilmer Building was the first building you would see. It was quite impressive then, and I think that it still is today.

A third Historic District in the city of Binghamton is the **State Street-Henry Street Historic District**. This district is very close to the downtown and includes approximately twenty buildings, and listed on the National Register of Historic Places in 1986. This section's anchors are two significant historical landmarks, The **Federal Courthouse and Post Office,** and the **Binghamton Republican-Herald Building**.

The **Binghamton Republican-Herald Building** was a newspaper building that housed three different newspapers. Now it has become a popular restaurant in the downtown area of Binghamton called Burger Mondays. The building also has apartments. The Federal Courthouse and Post Office building are still in use today but in different capacities.

The Binghamton Republican-Herald Building

The Federal Courthouse and Post Office.

Other prominent businesses on the street today include **Anthony Brunelli's Studio and Art Gallery**. Anthony Brunelli is an internationally renowned photorealist painter. He played a big part in the naming of State Street Artist's Row and the First Friday event. He lives in the same building as his art gallery.

Anthony Brunelli Fine Arts became established in the Historic District in 2003. Anthony Brunelli Fine Arts is a contemporary fine art gallery owned by Anthony Brunelli, under the directorship of his brother John Brunelli. You can expect to find the best examples of contemporary realism, photorealism, and well-disciplined abstract paintings. The art gallery also features drawings, sculpture, original prints, and alternative photographic media by international artists. Fine quality artisanship, labor-intensive production, and innovation are central to the gallery's program.

Anthony Brunelli's Studio and Art Gallery

Atomic Tom's is another art gallery and entertainment center on the street as well. If eleven-foot tin ceilings, intricate and beautiful chandeliers, handmade bar, French windows, and Mexican tile floors are what you need for a special event, then Atomic Tom's is your place.

Atomic Toms.

The last district I will mention is the **Abel Bennett Tract Historic District**. The area includes over 300 homes that are roughly north of Riverside Drive and spans several blocks scattered with beautiful residences built between 1890 and 1920. In 2008, the historic district became listed on the National Register of Historic Places. Too many to show, but if you take a leisurely drive down Riverside Drive, you cannot miss them!

Abel Bennett had the distinction of becoming the first mayor of Binghamton. The large area in the district is where he settled when he moved to the Village of Binghamton back in 1860. Abel also played a big part in the formation of the now defunct Binghamton Savings Bank and worked many years as the president of the First National Bank.

Abel bennet Tract.

These are just a few examples of the type of architecture we have surrounding us here. I love the architecture in Binghamton.

The **John E. Whitmore House** is a Queen-Anne-style dwelling constructed in 1888. The house has two- and one-half stories framed with irregular massing and brick. It has half-timber and Stucco and shingle exterior surfaces and listed on the National Register of Historic Places in 1986.

John E. Whitmore House

J. Stuart Wells House

HOME IS WHERE MY HEART IS

The construction of the **J. Stuart Wells House** occurred between 1867-1870. Noted New York State architect Isaac G. Perry designed the house. The structure is a two-and-a-half-story brick dwelling on a cut stone foundation and topped by a hipped, cross-gabled roof. The home expanded in 1940-1950 and featured a wrap-around porch. Also on the property is a two-story brick carriage house. It is now home to Parson's Funeral Home and listed on the National Register of Historic Places in 2009.

Gen. Edward F. Jones House

Gen. Edward F. Jones House is a historic home in Binghamton. They constructed the home in 1872 and is a large 2 ½ story, irregularly shaped building built of an eclectic combination of materials and textures. It was part of a large estate assembled by General Edward F. Jones (1828–1913). By 1883, they constructed the foundation and first floor of brick, while the upper stories are of wood with shingle, beaded board, and clapboard siding. It is an exceptional example of the Queen Ann style. The house became listed it on the National Register of Historic Places in 2005.

In 1861, Edward f jones joined the 6th Massachusetts Militia as a Major, and quickly assumed the rank of commander as a Colonel. He led the organization on its famed march through Baltimore. This battle was in the beginning of the American Civil War. His troops traveled onward and helped with the defense of Washington, D.C.

President Andrew Johnson nominated Jones for the grade of brevet brigadier general in 1866. He also served as Binghamton Police Commissioner and Lieutenant of New York.

The **Alfred Dunk House** is a very Historic house on Pine Street in Binghamton. This beautiful two-story home building took place in 1854 and included a stone basement and an attic. The house stands out from others with a steeply pitched roof that peaks in front boasting a beautiful ornate design.

They designed the building in the Carpenter Gothic style and listed on the National Registry of Historic Places in 1985.

The Alfred Dunk House on Pine Street in Binghamton.

Through the years, the Dunk House changed owners several times. Finally, in the 1980s, the house had a new owner who loved to bring old things back to life. Howard and Phyllis Brinker sold antiques. They bought the home and used one wing of the house serving as the shop. Howard became dedicated to the restoration of the house. He put back together the cherry banister that he found in pieces and restored brass fixtures on windows and doors that were original to the house. He even pieced back together the decorative woodwork that crowns the very top of the steep roof, which had shattered. The city rewarded his hard work with an award. When Howard's wife Phyllis died, he gifted the house to the Daughters of the American Revolution in her memory. The organization still owns the house today.

While I am speaking about older homes, here is another story that some friends want to share with you about our area.

The House on the Hill

There is a house on an east-side street that has a history of a haunted and mysterious nature. It was a beautiful home, gothic style, a mansion of sorts. As a young boy, I had heard haunted tales about that house. However, as a young girl, Sharon spent many a weekend there.

A family lived there at the time that she thought so highly of a second family. It was a large family comprising eight children, the mother who took care of her children while the father traveled extensively, gone for two weeks every month. The parents allowed all their eight children to invite a friend overnight every weekend. Sharon was one of those friends' that spent many weekends there.

It impressed her by how all eight of the children respected this home both inside and out. They kept the house in the same immaculate shape that it was in when they purchased it. Two rooms were off-limits to the children most of the time. One was the father's study, which had a beautiful white fluffy rug and probably the most prominent TV available. That room remained locked until the father came home. Then the children enjoyed sitting on that rug and watching tv. The other room was the mother's sitting room, her study. It was customary to see that both places remained locked.

It was a beautiful home that almost seemed like it had an entrance to the next street over at one time. As you explored, some of the home doors were leading downstairs that most of the children avoided to open. One room there had contained chains at one time.

The attic of the home was formerly a ballroom and was another area not entered very often.

The House on the Hill.

On the weekends, everyone fell asleep except for Sharon, as the children all gathered around upstairs to sleep. She tried to sleep, but the noises she heard from up in the attic kept her wide-eyed. She could listen to them, and the funny thing she found out later is that whenever someone went into the attic, the boxes stored up there always seemed to move to a different spot.

The attic fascinated her; one night, she sneaked over by the stairs to see if she could hear the noises better. Instead, she heard two voices carrying on a conversation. It was a matter-of-fact conversation that she could not quite make out the words. She asked the mother about the attic. The mother replied, "oh, that's nothing to worry about," and just smiled at her.

On another occasion, Sharon was upstairs in the room. She heard the call, "Dinner's ready!" On her way downstairs, she passed the mother's room, her study. To her surprise, the door was open, and she could hear a little girl giggling. The family's youngest daughter, Maureen, was the obvious choice of the giggling sound. The laugh seemed to come from under the mother's desk. Sharon says, "Maureen, you heard the call. Dinner's ready." There was no response, but still a faint sound of a silly little girl. So, Sharon says, "ok, well, I'm going down. See you later."

Sharon heads down to the kitchen through the stairway once used for the maid's quarters. She enters the kitchen, looking over the two picnic tables there they used for family meals. There sits Maureen!

"How did you get here before me, Maureen?" The rest of the children say, we have all been waiting for you. Maureen has been sitting here for ten minutes! Sharon told the mother about what had happened. The mother said to her that yes, there is a little girl who frequents the home. The mystery continues.

Thank you, Sharon Joy Shadduck, for sharing your story with us.

CHAPTER FIVE

CAROUSEL CAPITAL OF THE WORLD!

My son David and granddaughter Willa while riding the carousel.

Regarding Carousels, the Binghamton area has a rich history involving six carousels. Many people consider the Binghamton area the "Carousel Capital of the World!" Now, these carousels will not take you on a death-defying ride offering speed and upside-down loops and such. However, they will transport you back to a time when life was much more straightforward. They provided my children with many incredible pony rides.

One of the best features of these antique merry-go-rounds is that they are free! The only requirement asked to ride on a carousel is to donate one piece of litter! Imagine that! That is the way George F. Johnson wanted it, and that is the way it remains today. Each carousel contains beautifully restored horses and whirls to the beat of an old-time Wurlitzer organ. My children loved going to the parks, and while playing there, they always rode on the carousels.

From Memorial Day through Labor Day, take the time to visit the entire circuit of all six carousels. Carousel enthusiasts can earn an "I Rode the Carousel Circuit" button by turning in a card validated by park attendants at each of the carousel locations. It is a small thing, but to your children, it is a significant accomplishment. Please remember that if you did not complete the task as a child, it is never too late!

All six of the carousels donated to Broome County locations came from George W. Johnson, owner of the Endicott Johnson Shoe

Company. George F felt carousels contributed to a happy life and would help youngsters grow into reliable and productive citizens. His devotion to his workers, children, and family structure played a factor in my decision to stay here to raise my family.

The carousels in our area include the **Recreation Park Carousel, Ross Park Zoo Carousel, Charles F. Johnson Park Carousel, George W. Johnson Carousel, West Endicott Park Carousel, and Highland Park Carousel**. Here is a little history of the carousels in our area.

Recreation Park Carousel is in Binghamton, N.Y. George F. Johnson gifted this carousel to Binghamton for children and their families to enjoy back in 1925.

Recreation Park carousel.

The carousel has a sixteen-sided pavilion with a dome on top and features sixty horses for the children to ride and enjoy. The carousel also has two chariots and rotates to the beat of a beautiful Wurlitzer Military Band Organ. During the winter, Recreation Park Carousel is host to "Holiday Rides at Recreation Park" on Saturdays in December. Children and their families ride in the chill of winter during the holiday season.

In 2011, the carousel received a special honor when artists and filmmakers painted several prominent panels, Cortlandt Hull. The panels depict scenes from the Twilight Zone episodes To Serve Man, and it is a Good Life, Walking Distance, Time Enough at Last, The Howling Man, Living Doll, and A Stop at Willoughby. It was a unique way of honoring Rod Serling for Binghamton's love and the adventures that he had in the park as a child.

Ross Park Zoo Carousel is in Binghamton, N.Y. George F. Johnson gifted this carousel to Binghamton back in 1920. It was a donation for the location of the Ross Park Zoo. A wooden sixteen-sided pavilion surrounds the carousel with an eight-sided dome on top.

The carousel features sixty horses that stand four abreast (each one is a jumper) and has two chariots for the children to ride. Constructed by the Allan Herschell Co. of North Tonawanda and contains its original Wurlitzer #146-A Band Organ. The carousel became listed under the National Register of Historic Places in 1992.

C. Fred Johnson Park Carousel, in Johnson City, is the largest in our area and donated back in 1923. An enclosed wooden, two-story, eighteen-sided pavilion topped by a six-sided cupola surrounds the carousel. The carousel has seventy-two horses (each of which is a jumper), constructed by the Allan Herschell Company of North Tonawanda.

Ross Park Zoo Carousel.

This carousel was another gift to Johnson City from George F. Johnson, one of six that he donated to our region's children. They listed the carousel under the National Register of Historic Places back in 1992.

We highly decorated the CFJ carousel with holiday lights between Thanksgiving and Christmas and is open on weekends for the children and their families to ride.

George W. Johnson Park Carousel was in Endicott, N.Y., and donated back in 1934. An enclosed wooden, one-story, sixteen-sided pavilion surrounds the carousel. The carousel has thirty-six horses standing three abreast (each of which is a jumper) and two chariots. Constructed by the Allan Herschell Company of North Tonawanda and was another gift from George F. Johnson to the people here. They listed it under the National Register of Historic Places back in 1992.

CFJ Park Carousel, the giant carousel in our area.

This carousel presents "Halloween at the Scarousel" in October Halloween and "Little Italy Christmas" in December during the holidays for all visitors to enjoy. The location of the carousel is in a section of Endicott known as Little Italy.

George W. Johnson Park Carousel

West Endicott Park Carousel was in Endicott, N.Y., and donated back in 1929. An enclosed wooden, one-story, sixteen-sided enclosed pavilion surrounds the carousel. The carousel has thirty-four horses, one pig, one dog (each of which is a jumper), and two chariots. Constructed by the Allen Herschell Company of North Tonawanda and was another gift to George F. Johnson's people. They listed this carousel on the National Register of Historic Places back in 1992.

The West Endicott Park is next to Endicott-Johnson factories. A standing example of the commitment to providing recreational facilities for EJ employees. The West-Endicott Park has a kiddie pool, tennis courts, a playground, and a covered picnic shelter.

West Endicott Park Carousel.

Highland Park Carousel is in Endwell, N.Y. We also knew it as the EnJoie Park Carousel and the Ideal Park Carousel. They purchased this carousel between 1920 and 1925 and moved to its present site in 1967. An enclosed wooden, one-story, sixteen-sided enclosed pavilion surrounds the carousel. The carousel has thirty-four horses, one pig, one dog (each of which is a jumper), and two chariots. Constructed by the **Allan Herschell Company** of North Tonawanda and was another gift for George F. Johnson's people. They listed the carousel in the National Register of Historic Places back in 1992.

There are less than one-hundred seventy carousels left within the United States and Canada borders, and we have six of them right here in our area. I have always appreciated the tradition of things like this to benefit the people. Older traditions formed long ago helped to keep me in this area. I have an incredible feeling of pride from what the others that lived here before us felt about the Binghamton area. So, why are you waiting? Get on your horse and ride!

Highland Park Carousel.

Ride all six of the carousels and get your button!

CHAPTER SIX

BINGHAMTON PARKS AND MUSEUMS

Binghamton has quite a few parks within the city limits. They include **West End Park, Columbus Park, ACA Memorial Park, Valley Street Park, First Ward Park, Webster Street Park, Boland Park, Confluence Park, Recreation Park, Otsiningo Park, Cheri Lindsey Memorial Park, MacArthur Park, Fairview Park, and the Chenango River Walk**. Some are bigger than others and offer more activities. My wife and I spent many hours at the city parks with our children.

Binghamton Recreation Park is one of Binghamton's largest parks and offers outstanding tennis courts, a softball-little league field, and an old-time bathhouse leading into a beautiful public swimming pool. There is a lovely outdoor bandstand pavilion that offers summer concerts. Recreation Park also contains one of the six carousels in the triple city area, a Boy with Fish fountain statue that feeds into a small reflecting pool, several beautiful walking trails, and a statue of the park's founder George F. Johnson. Originally, the park also had a giant wooden toboggan slide, but unfortunately, a fire destroyed the slide years ago.

Before the park formed, the entire area was farmland. George F. Johnson purchased the eighteen acres plus back in 1921 and donated that land to Binghamton. His only demand was that it would remain as a public park forever. He asked the city of Binghamton to maintain the upkeep of the property. George F. gifted Allan Herschell Carousel with a Wurlitzer #146-B Band Organ to the city in 1925. I always felt that men like George F. Johnson enjoyed showing their love for family and children with his generosity. The devotion he showed became one reason that made me love this city as well.

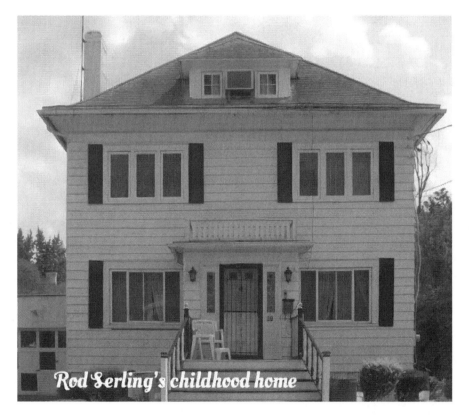

Rod Serling's childhood home is located just blocks from Recreation Park.

HOME IS WHERE MY HEART IS

Recreation Park was a favorite playing area for our famous Binghamton native, Rod Serling. Rod lived very close to Recreation Park. During his youth, he would run from his home to the park almost every day. Rod particularly enjoyed spending his time on the beautiful carousel, and Rod enjoyed the outdoor pavilion very much. Also, he would enjoy ice skating there in the park during the winter months. Ice skating has been missing from the park for a few years now. However, the skating rink has re-opened recently for all the children to enjoy.

The Twilight Zone "Walking Distance" plaque honors Rod Serling's devotion to the Binghamton area.

Rod Serling references the carousel in Recreation Park in one of the first episodes of his popular television series, The Twilight Zone. The television episode entitled "Walking Distance" became his way of honoring his hometown of Binghamton, N.Y.

As a child, he etched his initials into the outdoor pavilion where the bands would play. The insertion of a special plaque into the floor of the building is our way of honoring him. It is a beautiful bronze plaque that references Rod Serling and the special episode of the Twilight Zone.

Recreation Park Foundation.

Ice Skating is back! George F. Johnson Memorial.

Recreation Park Carousel and the Boy with Fish Fountain.

Recreation Park Carousel and the well-known Pavilion.

Recreation Park Pool and the gazebo leading into the playground.

My grandchildren, Madison and Ryan are enjoying the carousel during the holidays

The Holiday Carousel Rides is a yearly event at Recreation Park in December. The celebration offers carousel rides, hayrides,

Santa meets and greets, piano music in the Pavilion, singing from the All-Saints Chorus, and Horse and Buggy Rides. Hot chocolate for the crowd is also available. Just sit down, relax, and watch the carousel go around. The entire program is free and takes place three weekends in December.

Holiday Rides at Recreation Park, Carousel, and Pavilion.

Christmas Music in the Pavilion and the Holiday Horse and Buggy Sleigh Rides

Cheri Lindsey Memorial Park is one of my favorite parks in Binghamton. I invested many years coaching our youth, girls' softball, on the east side of Binghamton. We traveled to the north side of Binghamton to play the teams based at Cheri Lindsey Memorial Park. I became more involved with coaching the girls, as we had three daughters growing up here.

Back in 1984, the Binghamton City Council unanimously approved the name change to Cheri Lindsey Memorial Park. It is a very fitting name in the memory of a beautiful young and vibrant twelve-year-old girl brutally murdered during that time. Cheri played softball in that park, and I believe she was a catcher. I felt honored to coach some games there every year. We played against the teams honored with her name on their shirts.

Cheri's parents held raffles in her memory throughout the years and used the money raised to pay it forward to Binghamton's City. They had events in her honor that included a block party at the park and became involved with purchasing and installing lighting on the baseball field. Cheri Lindsey Park now has lights installed that provide the ability to play night games. They supported our youth by sponsoring boys' little league teams and girls' softball teams for many years.

The honor of the memories of those who lived here is one reason I never moved away. To me, it just instilled the feeling of community deep inside my heart. This city, to me, just feels like family.

Beautiful Public Art honoring the memory of Cheri Lindsey and below is the entrance to the skating facility.

Skateboarding at Cheri Lindsey Park!

This beautiful park includes a large skate park, a dog park, a public swimming pool, walking trails, a lighted field for softball and Little League games, concession stand, restrooms, playground area for the children, basketball courts and offers picturesque views of the Chenango River as part of the Chenango Riverwalk. There are beautiful murals painted on the buildings throughout the park, including Cheri's beautiful painting herself. A beautiful tribute to a little girl who was so full of life!

Otsiningo Park is a name derived from the American Indian in the lower Chenango River. Otsiningo Park offers the community multiple soccer and softball fields, sand volleyball courts, a large children's playground, community gardens, picnic facilities, and a trail along the Chenango River's wooded bank. However, that is just a small part of what the park provides for the city here.

Otsiningo Park has held a SpiedieFest and Balloon Rally event every year for the last thirty-five years. The highlight of the three-day event is judging the area's best spiedies, a food delicacy born here. Also, balloon launches twice a day, entertainment, and music for all to enjoy. It is also a great time to shop for various crafts from the area.

Each year, the park holds a Scarecrow display contest. A fun event that anyone can enter. Individuals, families, businesses, clubs, groups, and organizations may join. The entry is free. Great project to do as a fun family event!

Nature surrounds you at Otsiningo Park.

Otsiningo Park hosts the annual scarecrow Contest.

Otsiningo Park hosts the annual scarecrow Contest.

Otsiningo Park hosts the annual scarecrow Contest.

Otsiningo Park hosts the annual scarecrow Contest.

Another great event takes place throughout the summer in Otsiningo Park, Broome Bands Together. A free summer concert series where you can grab your lawn chair and head out to the park to listen to the bands play. All the concerts held at Otsiningo Park are in the early evening hours during June and July. The shows are free for the public. Straw hats and lemonade are optional!

Balloon launching from Otsiningo Park is a familiar sight during the summer!

Otsiningo Park, Music in the summer!

There is always something to do at Otsiningo Park.

Fairview Park is a park where I spent many summers. Our family included three daughters that all played softball and a son who played in the Little League. I became heavily involved in Fairview Park for about thirteen years. I coached girls' softball for that period for the City of Binghamton and a local support group called East Side Youth Association. Those years of service are years I will never forget. My wife volunteered to help as well. It made me feel like I was giving back to my hometown and its youth in a small way.

Fairview Park carries on some traditions on the east side of Binghamton. The park features tennis courts, a swimming pool, a playground area, basketball courts, a Little League field, and a Softball Field. It is common to see softball and little league tournaments playing games there during the summer months.

The very first Dick's Sporting Goods store in Binghamton.

As I have mentioned, this book is about never forgetting your roots. Some believe this area is not a great place to get employment. Great businesses have started here in Binghamton. The very first Dick's Sporting Goods Store opened here. This great business created many job opportunities. Back in the day, I went to school with Tim, Kim, and Ed. It heavily involved two families with the success that Dick's Sporting Goods stores now have across the country. Tim Myers was a driver at our wedding. His wife Kim (daughter of Dick's Sporting Goods owner) was a customer of mine when I sold advertising for the Press & Sun-Bulletin local newspaper, and Ed

Stack (Owner's son) and I played football together. All three are fellow Binghamton North High classmates.

They are all great people, and you may wonder why I bring them up when talking about Fairview Park. I bring them up because they are a perfect example of the extraordinary people that did not forget their roots. The two families committed on behalf of Dick's Sporting Goods this fall. They have committed to upgrading both the little league and softball fields at Fairview Park! The city of Binghamton thanks them, as do many others who live here, to give back to our community.

Sometimes when talking about where we live, we lose sight of who made a difference in our area. I am proud to attach an extraordinary story to a special man in the history of Fairview Park. His name was Fred Schneider.

The man leaned on the fence at Button Field in Fairview Park on the East Side of Binghamton one night in 1968, watching boys play Little League Baseball.

The man asked the league supervisor what would occur in this field of dreams for the little girls? Maybe he was thinking about his daughter Brenda and the other East Side girls without teams or games.

The man was Fred Schneider, and soon Fred was the leader in the East Side Youth Association Girls Softball program, which was the forerunner of the Binghamton Recreation girls set ball programs all over the city.

Once Fred got involved in softball, he never let up. He was, first, a teacher/coach, then a manager, a volunteer umpire, a groundskeeper, a concessionaire, a commissioner, and the first youth softball commissioner for the ASA in the state of New York.

As the State Youth Commissioner, it was common for Fred to pack up wife Emma and the family in the car, and off they would go to give a clinic for coaches at some place like Utica—all the time selling ASA Softball and teaching how to play the game.

In 1972, Fred was a director of the first Broome County Girls Softball Tournament at Button Field. Many more were to follow as the Southern Tier moved far ahead of other counties in the state with the youth programs.

Fred became a nationally known figure in the ASA as his attendance at the National conventions brought him into essential developments in the youth programs across the states.

Fred was selling Binghamton as a National Tournament City. His bid presentations brought the best softball players in the world to play on Binghamton area diamonds. Fred got the tournament bid; he was the co-director of all the Nationals with his East Side partner/Commissioner Carl Gaffney.

We remember Fred in the concession stand frying hamburgers and the stove exploding. An ambulance whisked Fred to General Hospital only to see Fred return in 45 minutes because he did not have time to wait for treatment.

In 1975, a heart ailment forced him to retire. Did he slow down? Never. Now, there was just more time to work on softball as he continued to coach three teams along with his wife, plus umpiring at Button Field, where another ambulance one hot day carted away the umpire behind the plate. He avoided the limelight. Fred would never get in a team picture. He wanted no attention. Regardless, the New York State ASA made him one of the first selections to the Hall of Honor in 1987. The same year, the New York State ASA Scholarship Award has renamed the Fred Schneider Memorial Scholarship Award.

His heart finally gave out late at night on April 22, 1987, while Fred was driving to the Binghamton post office with a load of softball mail. He was 53.

Thank you, Fred Schneider. Rest in Peace.

(Note: An excerpt from the Fred Schneider Memorial Classic program of July 1991.)

I enjoyed coaching the City of Binghamton softball teams. The girls that I coached were all great children who just wanted to be part of a team. They wanted to learn how to play softball. The

Binghamton City league was a way for our city to give these children a place to learn about the game.

I enjoyed it because it was not about tournament team softball, although some girls did so. The game and the fun of the game were what it was about. Children could be part of a team with a goal. It was not about winning or losing; It was about getting out and smelling the fresh-cut grass. During the game, you cheered for your friends and teammates. It was about sharing bubble gum with your teammates in the dugout. It was about getting together after the game and sharing stories while enjoying an ice cream cone.

I loved the game then, and I still do today. It was a game that I wish I played baseball as a kid. When I coached, I was a kid again!

There are parks on every side of this city. Parks formed for one reason and one reason only. Parks made for our children to have a place to gather and play. They made it to represent a community that cares about the families that live here. Some parks are memorials to brave men and women who gave their lives to help others. We do not forget them. We remember the brave police and firefighters who have served this city and the innocent people who died for no reason. We recognize children like Cheri Lindsey. People like the workers in the American Civic Association passed on for no reason at all.

The ACA Memorial Park includes a vertical broken column to symbolize a life cut short. Bird sculptures placed on posts in an arrangement suggestive of a flock disturbed and flying away. Memorial plaques with text and graphics designed by each family, a surrounding garden of roses and evergreens, and using a tree that existed at the final site. A quiet place tucked away with our city to honor these beautiful people who lost their lives for no apparent reason during a mass shooting.

This memorial is a remembrance of one of the deadliest mass shootings in United States history. The deadly event took place at the American Civic Association on April 3rd, 2009. He killed fourteen people on that day. Innocent English students and teachers in a classroom at the center became victims of the shooting. The shooter blocked the back door with his car and entered the front of the building, and began his killing spree. After he completed this terrible act, he turned the gun on himself and committed suicide.

ACA Memorial Park.

We never received a good reason for the shooting. However, those who knew him felt the reason was the difficult circumstances he faced as an immigrant to this country motivated him.

Some very interesting information I discovered while writing this book was the location of the Martin Luther King Jr. Promenade and Peacemaker's Stage. Binghamton honored the famous civil rights activist with the addition of these well-deserved memorials. We built the stage at the approximate location of the Knickerbocker Building. That building was the headquarters of the New York Ku Klux Klan organization during the 1920s.

Martin Luther King Memorial and Promenade

So, how did Binghamton get the distinction of becoming the headquarters of this terrible racist organization? Well, the obvious choice for New York State was New York City. However, New York City had a large immigrant population that included big numbers of Catholics and Jewish. Putting the headquarters for New York State there received much negativity from the people. The search was on for a location where it would be a better fit. Upstate New York seemed to be a better fit for the headquarters location and the KKK felt there were better opportunities to recruit members here.

There were several reasons Binghamton came to their attention. Binghamton at the time was a city that had a small percentage of foreign-born residents and that people here had many conservative values. The Klan had purchased a headquarters on the intersection of Wall and Henry Street.

The national organization wanted ownership of that headquarters location, but the local Klan leadership did not want to give it up. So, they eliminated the Binghamton site from the national organization. The location in Binghamton failed to survive on its own and the national organization pulled their charter.

I feel so proud of my city that they chose this location to honor Martin Luther King, and all he stood for. Bravo Binghamton, well played indeed.

Dr. Martin Luther King Memorial Promenade.

If you walk from the Martin Luther King Promenade stage toward the entrance of the promenade, you will find a memorial marker. The marker is to honor those who lost their lives in the July 22nd, 1913 Binghamton Clothing Company Fire. Thirty-one people died that day in one of the worst tragedies by fire in Binghamton's history. There is also a memorial in the Spring Forest Cemetery in Binghamton.

Binghamton certainly has our share of impressive museums, and they are a big part of the community. The museums include The Phelps Mansion Museum, Roberson Mansion Museum, and Science Center, Bundy Museum of History and Art, Techworks, Ross Park Zoo, Discovery Center of the Southern Tier, and the Binghamton University Art Museum.

HOME IS WHERE MY HEART IS

One of the most famous museums in Binghamton is the Roberson Mansion Museum and Science Center. The Roberson Mansion is part of the Roberson Museum and Science Center. This mansion still stands tall near downtown Binghamton, built with the Italian Renaissance style, and designed by a Binghamton architect named C. Edward Vosbury. The building of the estate started in 1904 but did not complete until 1907. Alonzo Roberson Jr. and his wife Margaret Hays Roberson would make the mansion their home. The building contained all the then-modern conveniences available. The installation included modern amenities such as an elevator, central heat, combination gas, electric lighting, a dumbwaiter, an intercom system, and a private bath for each bedroom. Hard to believe such luxuries meant so much in that day and time.

The New York City interior design firm, Pottier & Stymus, designed the interior decorations. They chose the Townsend & Fleming landscape firm from Buffalo to do the grounds. Titchener Ironworks designed and manufactured the wrought-iron fence that surrounds the building. Many say the mansion may contain the ghost of its former owner, Alonzo Roberson. Many believe his spirit still roams around the estate. His apparitions appear in the elevator and along the upper corridors of the mansion.

Roberson Museum and Science Center.

The Roberson Museum and Science Center is located just to the right of the estate. The museum's exhibits focus on art, local history, science, and natural history. A planetarium is also in the museum. The planetarium has many shows dealing with astronomy, outer space, planets, and much more. The museum features changing exhibits and a large model train layout that depicts regional landscapes from the 1950s. That display is where you can get a peek at how Binghamton looked in the past.

The museum also hosts annual special events. They include decorating the Roberson Mansion for the Christmas holidays, a food and wine festival, Halloween activities, science fiction conventions (like a Robocon event), a model train and doll fair, and much more.

Roberson's Museum displays an annual Christmas Tree Display!

Roberson's Museum displays an annual Christmas Tree Display!

Roberson's Museum displays an annual Christmas Tree Display!

Well, I hope you did not think I was going to skip that haunted

part, did you? I asked around to see if anyone had some interesting stories to share. Several friends agreed to share some experiences. Here we go, get your spook on!

Things "Happen" at the Roberson Museum

Keri had some strange events at Roberson that she agreed to share with you. I used to work in the planetarium at Roberson. I created and presented the planetarium shows to both the public and private groups. Part of the job was doing slide photography and creating slides for the presentation, so I spent a lot of time building when no shows were going on. I spent time in the planetarium, the offices above the museum, and down in the darkroom developing film and creating slides.

The house originated with a small wrought iron elevator in it. One time I took the elevator up to where some offices are. I got in, turned around, and pushed the button for the floor I wanted. After the doors closed, I took a step back and bumped into someone. It felt like I bumped into a real person standing behind me, but I was alone in the elevator, and I did not back up into the wall. When I finished, I apologized to whoever was behind me and to the stairs back down!

I went in early on a Sunday morning to prepare for the new show that was starting. I came into the building through the security office since the building was not open yet. The only other people in the building were the two security guards. I headed to the planetarium and let myself in. As the door closed behind me, I heard piano music coming from the theater, so I put my stuff in the office and went back to check it out. I could clearly hear the piano up on the stage playing from outside the theater doors. When I opened the door, the music stopped, and there was no one at the keyboard or in the room. It was dark except for the safety lights, and there was no one anywhere in the theater. I walked around and checked the back rooms and even went and called security to check with them. No one had been in there. There were many other times I was there alone and heard that piano, but after that, I just left whoever's spirit alone to play the piano.

One of the private events we used to host was for Girl Scouts to earn badges in science. We would have several trips sign up and have around 100 girl scouts, plus their leaders come to stay overnight at the museum. They would steady until midnight working on all kinds of fun science projects to earn badges. They would camp out in the theater and have breakfast in the morning before a little badge ceremony and heading home. I used to stay overnight and help one of the science program leaders run all the projects. I always slept in the planetarium or the planetarium office. There were many nights I would hear the outer door open and the sound of footsteps, but there would be no one around. I would get up and do a walk-through in the science section and the theater, but everything was always quiet.

They also involved me in Roberson's helping a theater group put on shows in the theater. I cannot remember the group's name, but they put on shows like Hair and A Chorus Line. I would help with costumes, lighting, sound, wherever they needed help. There were lots of little things that would happen during a show. Pieces of costumes would disappear and reappear in different places or the next day. We disconnected cords, and when we came in the next day, we witnessed the same cables now connected! Sometimes lights would go if in one of the dressing rooms upstairs while people were using it. They always tried to warn us about other theater groups that used the theater because you still left the two front row center seats empty. The supervision instructed us NEVER to sell those tickets for a performance. There was one performance that I was part of where the chairs sold accidentally, and we had nothing but problems throughout the show. One actor received an injury. Lighting equipment fell, props went missing. We always made sure those seats remained empty after that!

Thank you for sharing your experiences with us, Keri Cook Spencer

Who Slammed the Window?

As parents, we all remember our infamous school bus trips. Parents and children alike getting so excited to get on that bus and whisked off to a new adventure.

It was a hot summer day when the school planned the trip. She went along on the trip as a chaperone to help the teachers with the children. Her son was in the second grade, and his class was going to tour the Roberson Museum.

They proceeded through the museum with everything going along just fine until they reached the area of Mr. Roberson's office was. The class was now on the very top floor of the museum. If you decide to tour the museum now, that same area converted to the new grand ballroom. She had taken pictures along the way to capture the memory of her son and classmates. As the class entered his office's former area, she noticed something that she felt could be very dangerous for the children. Linda noticed an open window. These windows were old-fashioned gable styled with no screen. They positioned the windows from the floor up, meaning that the window presented a threat that a child could slide under the window and fall to the ground. As a concerned parent and worrying about the children's welfare, she went over to the window and closed it. She double-checked the lock to make sure.

Feeling a bit more relieved now, she continued taking pictures while also assisting the teachers with the children. As the last child walked past the area where she had locked the window, there was a loud noise. It was the sound as if someone had kicked in the door. To their amazement, the shutters on that window (although locked) had swung open and smashed against the outer brick wall. The day was calm. There was no wind at all. The class left the area with a bit of confusion about the incident.

Before this trip, she had no knowledge that there was a haunted history at the Roberson Museum. The entire experience they had there played out that evening when she had the pictures printed. In one child's photograph, she noticed something as they walked through the museum towards her. In that picture, there was a white orb right behind the very last child in line, the same child that passed the window before the loud smash.

There was no doubt in her mind that she had a spiritual experience that day! That event was a spooky story that she will never forget!

Thank you for sharing your experience with us, Linda Healey King

Faces in the Dark!

The best source for the spookiest stories comes from those of us that work at a well-known "haunted" location. The following story comes from a good friend of one of my daughters. Again, we travel back to the Roberson Museum. Her friend Michelle worked at the museum for many years. Often, as part of her duties had the job of opening and closing the museum.

Roberson Museum had that haunted history behind it, which always made her feel kind of creepy. However, it was part of the job, and she found it helped just to remind herself this was just a big old scary house. Often, she even spoke to the museum as a person by saying "good morning" or "good night" as she closed the museum down for the day.

It well known Roberson Museum for its Christmas displays. During the holidays, the museum offers unique tours of the museum, displaying Christmas themes worldwide. They say Mr. Roberson seems to appear the most at the museum around the closing time in the evenings.

Look in the doorway below the light in the room.

One night during the holiday season, Michelle was the last employee to leave, so she had locked up and turning Christmas scenes off for the night. As she entered each area to turn lights off and close things up, she stopped to take a picture of all the beautiful Christmas displays like so many others have done.

Michelle was unaware of something in one picture that she noticed later as she looked over all the pictures. In one photo, she was pretty sure she captured something out of the ordinary. Under a light in one image, she saw what she really thought resembled the face of a man.

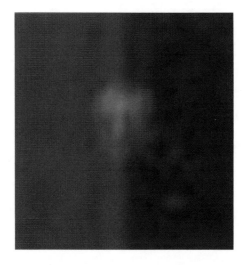

The image, when enhanced, resembles a man's face!

This likeness freaked her out. She could not believe it! In the attached picture, if you look closely under the light, you can see what, to me, seems like the face of a man. If you magnify that area of the photo, it becomes even more noticeable.

Other events that took place while Michelle worked there also occurred while she was closing the museum. She would enter a specific exhibit where there were televisions on. As Michelle closed the museum, it would be necessary to turn each of the TVs off. After doing this, if she walked close to that same exhibit, the televisions would all turn back on! Shaken and somewhat scared, she left the TVS on and ran out of that room. That event took place after her Christmas picture encounter.

Thank you for sharing your experience with us, Michelle Lynn Butts.

Excuse Me?

Here is another Roberson story that will make you scratch your head. This event also happened during an open tour in Roberson. You could go anywhere in the spacious mansion. Sharon went up the beautiful staircase that would take you upstairs to the area where the bedrooms would have been.

She turned the corner and entered one bedroom, and became shocked to see a man and a woman standing there. The couple were very prim and proper, and they both had a startled look on their faces. It seemed as if Sharon was intruding. These were images and not real people. What surprised her the most was the clothes they wore? The clothing was not from the time of the mansion and yet not of our time either. The images disappeared, and she went on the rest of the tour.

Before she left, she mentioned to two workers there what she had noticed. With the descriptions that she provided, it was a direct match to the former owners of the mansion, Alonzo Roberson, and his wife! It did not surprise them at all! The vision was not the first time that a visitor saw the couple.

Thank you for sharing your experience with us, Sharon Joy Shadduck.

They built the Phelps Mansion in 1870 as the private home of Sherman D. Phelps. Mr. Phelps was a successful businessperson, banker, Republican elector for Abraham Lincoln, and mayor of the City of Binghamton. Phelps hired Isaac Perry to design the new home and John Stewart Wells became the primary contractor for the mansion project. They completed Phelps Mansion at an estimated cost of $119,000. My guess is that today's equivalent would be about two-million dollars.

In 1872, "Judge" Phelps moved into his new home. That same year, he won election as mayor of the new town of Binghamton. The three-floor Second Empire-style home included a full kitchen and cook's apartment in the cellar. The first floor had a variety of rooms for entertainment. There was also a kitchen, parlor, dining room, formal waiting area, and solarium. The second floor contained the family's five bedrooms, a sitting room, and two bathrooms. Its interior features large rooms, thirteen- and one-half foot ceilings, magnificent chandeliers, walnut, rosewood, maple and golden oak woods, and a soaring black walnut staircase. A third floor included a billiard room, servants' rooms, and storage. Today, the third floor does not exist.

At the time Judge Phelps moved into the mansion, the household included himself, two teen-aged sons from his second marriage, a widowed niece who acted as social hostess, two farm girls who served as house cleaners, and freed slaves who served as carriage drivers and cooks.

Judge Phelps died in 1878 of Fells Disease. They laid him in state on the first floor of the mansion. Following his death, Judge Phelps' sons, Robert Sherman, and Arthur Davis, lived in the house for a time. Arthur died on October 30, 1880, and Robert died in 1881. Robert's widow, Harriett "Hattie" Storey Taylor Phelps, had lifetime use of the estate and lived in the mansion until her death in 1882.

They passed the estate on to Judge Phelps' nieces and nephews, none of whom wanted to live in the house. The mansion sat empty for several years and maintained by Andrew Jackson, a freed slave who had served the family as carriage driver for many years.

In 1889, they sold the mansion to George Harry Lester, a local shoe manufacturer. Mr. Lester was purchasing land near Binghamton to develop Lestershire, which is now known as Johnson City to enlarge his factory. Unfortunately, he encountered financial difficulties, and they sold the mansion at an auction.

John Stewart Wells, the original contractor, purchased the mansion and rented it to the James Christopher Truman family. They lived in the home until about 1905 when Mr. Truman retired from his position as the postmaster.

The Monday Afternoon Club, a women's civic organization. purchased the mansion in 1905. The club constructed a large ballroom at the back of the mansion in 1905. In 1986, they transferred ownership of the mansion to The Phelps Mansion Foundation. The New York State Board of Regents charted the Phelps Mansion as a museum in 2005.

Phelps Mansion and Museum

The Monday Afternoon Club disbanded in 2006 and transferred the ownership of the home and contents to the Phelps Mansion Museum.

They listed Phelps Mansion in the National Register of Historical Places in 1988. The Museum remains open and offers a variety of programs and regularly scheduled guided tours.

They Were Coming Right at Me!

At the Phelps Mansion, a friend of mine wanted to share a story with you regarding strange happenings. It was an event at Phelps Mansion on a winter night. Sharon attended the social gathering with a friend. It was the type of activity that started with a lovely dinner, followed by a break, and then the evening's main event in the ballroom. During the break, the mansion personnel allowed you to tour the building at your leisure until the evening's central portion started.

Many of the attendees wandered around the mansion, looking at all the beautiful reminders of life in the past. Sharon's friend went in another direction, but Sharon ended up going upstairs. She ended up going into a room there that she thought would have been Mr. Phelps's study. As Sharon cautiously entered the room, a noise started. She heard what sounded like metal plates on the tip of toes, a sound that seemed to get closer and closer. Sharon was alone and knew it was not her. No one else was near her.

Again, she hears that same sound. It was the type of tapping that you would associate with a man's dress shoe. Suddenly, the room went silent. She just had the feeling that she was not alone. It created a feeling like there were a few people in the room. She could almost sense the personalities of the crowd. She could see nothing or anyone, but just knew that she was not alone.

She nervously fumbled to get her camera and took this picture of the room in front of her. Astounded to see the number of orbs in the image, and they were all coming towards her! That is all she needed to know. Sharon quickly turned and left the area.

One thing rumored about the Phelps Mansion is the story of the clock on the mantle. One of the main rooms on the first floor, mixed in with all the other items from the past, is a beautiful timepiece. It is the type of clock that needs winding for it to work correctly. The people working in the mansion do not touch or turn the clock. However, mysteriously, when some people are touring the palace, it runs on its own.

One day while Sharon was visiting there, she passed that area and heard a clicking noise. She looked over at the clock, and it was running! Shocked and in awe, she turned towards the guide and asked if they heard that noise. The person said yes and shrugged their shoulders, merely saying, "it happens!"

Thanks for sharing your experience with us, Sharon Joy Shadduck.

The Harlow E. Bundy House, which is now known as the Bundy Museum of History and Art is still standing strong since 1892. The historical house was a home for Harlow, his wife, and their children for thirteen years until 1905. When manufacturing was at its peak in the area, the museum tells an interesting story.

Willard Bundy while working as a jeweler in Auburn, N.Y. and invented a time clock at forty-three years of age. The year was

1888. As time went on, he developed patents on many of the mechanical parts. A year later, his brother Harlow joined forces with Willard. They referred the time clocks to as "Bundy's" or "Bundy Clocks."

The business eventually incorporated to form the Bundy Manufacturing Company. They became the first business in the world to produce time clocks. The Bundy Manufacturing Company was off and running with a skeleton crew and very little capital. Willard and Harlow eventually had a fallout. Willard moved to Syracuse and started his own business, and Harlow continued to manage the Bundy Manufacturing Company. Harlow, in time developed an adding machine. As time passed, the company continued to grow. In 1924, through a series of acquisitions and mergers became an integral part of International Business Machines or IBM as we know it today.

The house itself was something to behold. If we built the same house today, I know the cost would be over one million dollars. the location is on 129 Main Street in Binghamton and became listed in the U.S. National Register of Historical Places in 2011. The museum is two and a half stories high and Harlow had the frame built using the British architectural Queen Ann Style. It features a decorative cut stone veneer and uses several styles of shingles. The feature on the building that I like the most is the cone shaped tower on the right front side of the building. In 2004, the home became a museum and served as a location for many activities.

The Bundy Museum of History and Art is a great showcase of the Victorian era housing and the life of the Bundy's inventions. A highlight of the museum is a recreation of the 1893 World Fair Booth, that displayed a variety of the time clocks made by the Bundy Manufacturing Company. The museum also has various exhibits of local history and art that change from time to time. There is a 20th century barber shop room on display where men gathered to talk while waiting to get their haircut. The museums open art gallery is for upcoming and established artists. They devoted a section to the Southern Tier Broadcasters Hall of Fame, honoring talents of Rod Serling, Richard Deacon and Bill Parker. The museum also hosts the Rod Serling Archive, with original wire images, TV and film props, memorabilia, and personal items.

Another exciting part supported by the museum is WBDY-LP 99.5 FM. "The Bundy" is a non-commercial community radio station devoted to enriching the Binghamton area's artistic and intellectual life. The station is a platform for local program hosts and the community to share their passions, knowledge, art, and perspective with Broome County and the national community radio listeners.

Check their website bundymuseum.org for information on museum tours. Here is a haunted tale from the Bundy Museum.

Sir, Your Horse and Carriage Awaits!

It seems like all the museums here have a mysterious side to them. The Bundy Museum of History and Art is no exception. Sharon had an experience while touring this museum as well. The museum has tours during the day, but she was attending an evening tour on this occasion.

Sharon's attention shifted to a room located towards the main floor back at the building's end. She was looking around in that area, which had a glass door leading to what looked like a side entrance. It was twilight so you could see outside even though it was a strain on your eyes. Out of the corner of her eye, she could see an image. She rubbed her eyes, making sure it was not her imagination.

Looking again through that glass, she sees a horse and buggy arrive outdoors, and a man with dark clothing exits the carriage. The man approached the building and disappeared into thin air. Sharon could not believe it! She went on with the tour, never mentioning what she saw in that window. However, with curiosity getting the better of her before she left, she asked the guide about that back-door area. He told her that back in the old days, that area is where the carriages would come in!

Thanks for sharing your experience with us, Sharon Joy Shadduck.

The Binghamton University Art Museum is a part of Binghamton University's campus in the Fine Arts building on the second floor. Over three thousand five hundred works, from various eras and different media types are in the Art Museum. The museum comprises paintings, sculptures, prints, photographs, drawings, glass, ceramic, metalwork, manuscript pages, and textiles.

Some of these beautiful art pieces come from faraway places Egypt, Greece, Asia, Africa, Europe, North America, and Pre-Columbian cultures. In recent years, the University Art Museum began an active campaign to share its collection with the public. This activity serves the university and our community by showing its commitment to education here. The museum is just another example of how Binghamton continues to commit to the arts.

Welcome to the Binghamton University Art Museum entrance.

Lithograph photo courtesy of Binghamton University Art Museum

TechWorks! is in the vintage Binghamton Ice Cream Company factory, built in 1912, expanded in 1946 and 1972, on the waterfront in downtown Binghamton, at 321 Water Street, Binghamton, and just north of two historic railroad trestles. Look for the colorful flood wall mural - Four Seasons Along the Chenango painted by JoAnne Arnold.

The 30,000 square foot vintage brick ice cream factory renovation with include new additions of the South Entrance Energy Exhibit showing emerging technologies, a rooftop River View Terrace, and the Garden of Ideas, a sculpture park in the forecourt. Renovations are starting from the inside out. The proposed exterior will look like this model.

Model of the new front portion of Techworks!

Development of TechWorks! is a Center initiative to highlight central New York State technology in action. Significant progress is underway collecting and revitalizing icons of 20th & 21st century U.S. technology in the Hall of Ones and Zeroes. The Vintage IBM Computing Center, including the only operational IBM 1401 mainframe on public display world-wide. Techworks features the Link Simulation Workshop that includes the Apollo Lunar Module Simulator, on long-term restoration and display loan from the Smithsonian's National Air and Space Museum.

The mission of the **Techworks** is to preserve documentation and display in context the inventions and industrial innovations of New York's Southern Tier.

They have done such a great job. Techworks won an International Award! They won the Tony Sale Award. To quote the reason from the judges, *"The team has brought back to life flight simulators from the 1940s, '1960's and '1980's which allow the public to experience them and to grasp the pace of innovation and development of simulation technology."*

The main feature in the museum has been the Link Flight Simulator. The simulators were a vital tool to teach pilots how to fly and used by our armed forces in that capacity. That is one reason Binghamton has earned the distinction of "the birthplace of virtual reality."

The museums here are great, but what about the children? What could Binghamton offer for the children and their families to do?

We can do what many others do from Binghamton. We can go to the Binghamton Zoo at Ross Park! Many in the area do not realize that the Ross Park Zoo is the fifth oldest zoo in the United States! My wife spent so many days with our children there. It is a great family place to unwind and relax.

The Binghamton Ross Park Zoo officially opened in 1875. The only cities with an older Zoo would rank to start with Philadelphia, Chicago, Cincinnati, and Buffalo. Erastus Ross, another very prominent wealthy businessperson, donated the ninety-acre plot of land to Binghamton. All that he asked was that the area becomes a park for all the community to enjoy.

Older Zoo Crowds, Photo Courtesy of Ross Park Zoo Staff

Originally, the park had a roller coaster, swings, and various other amusements that drew large crowds in our area. They erected the stone pillars in 1896 that welcomed visitors as they arrived. Can you just imagine families crowding into the park? They came to the zoo back then on carriages or a trolley.

2019 Red Panda - Photo Courtesy of Ross Park Zoo Staff

Ross Park Zoo had its first bear exhibit in 1919. During the same year, they received a donation from one of our famous carousels. Also, the zoo installed its first children's train ride called the Cannonball Express. That next train called the Ross Park Special replaced the cannonball Express, and in 2016, The Binghamton Zoo Express made its debut at the zoo.

Children were riding on the old helicopter ride. Photo courtesy of Ross Park Zoo Staff.

The Binghamton Zoo currently takes part in several of AZA's Species Survival Plan programs. Several of the animals living here have become critically endangered. We can visit some of these animals at the zoo, including the African Pancake Tortoise, African Penguin, Amur Leopard, Black-and-white Ruffed Lemur, Black Howler Monkey, Cinereous Vulture, Cougar, Fennec Fox, Fishing Cat, Geoffroy's Marmoset, Golden-headed Lion Tamarin, Green Aracari, Prehensile-tailed Porcupine, Red-necked Wallaby, Red Panda, Red Wolf, Snow Leopard, Snowy Owl, Southern Three-banded Armadillo*, Spotted-necked Otter, Two-toed Sloth, and the Wood Turtle.

Amur Leopard - Photo Courtesy of Ross Park Zoo Staff

Under the Southern Tier Zoological Society, Ross Park has undergone tremendous changes. The old blacktop paths, concrete surroundings, and steel bars have disappeared. Now you can enjoy your walkthrough to the zoo, traveling through the winding wooded roads with naturalistic exhibits that house over one hundred different species of animals.

The First Train, Cannonball Express - Photo Courtesy of Ross Park Zoo Staff

Sloth WE - Photo Courtesy of Ross Park Zoo Staff

2019 Zoomobile - Photo Courtesy of Ross Park Zoo Staff

Ross Park Zoo Carousel - Photo Courtesy of Ross Park Zoo Staff

The Binghamton Zoo at Ross Park is, without a doubt, a fun place to spend time together as a family. We spent many days there with our children. Time spent at the zoo created unforgettable memories for my family, especially for my children with their mom.

In 2015, the City of Binghamton completed the brand-new Ross Park Amphitheater. Adults and children can now enjoy various events sponsored by the Binghamton Zoo at Ross Park and Discovery Center of the Southern Tier.

Within the historic Binghamton Ross Park Zoo, is another great place to bring our children. The Discovery Center, this building is an interactive children's museum. This large facility of over twenty-three thousand square feet holds over thirty exhibits. They created displays for one reason: our children. Children even helped to build some of them!

The Discovery Center is an excellent place for children to learn and explore while having the ability to touch and manipulate items within the exhibits. Overall, this is a happy place for children to go to have fun! Finally, a place where parents can take their children to and relax. Why? Because here you do not have to tell your children, "Don't touch that!"

The Story Book Garden is a favorite stop for children!

Recent improvements include adding exhibit space, classrooms, a performance space, and enhancing visitor services. The museum also has made the necessary ADA accessibility features. Also, a new award-winning Story Garden outdoor exhibit space is just waiting for your children. This area focuses on families spending time together. Here families can read books, become a part of each outdoor exhibit, and enjoy the nature that surrounds them. You can even relax and eat your picnic basket of goodies in this area as well.

Johnny Hart's famous BC Caveman and Blossom the Bull.

HOME IS WHERE MY HEART IS

Discovery Center's Story Garden and Blossom the Bull.

Discovery Center's exhibits provide fun for the children.

Discovery Center's exhibits provide fun for the children.

Do you remember the Vestal Steakhouse Bull? This is the same bull.

Children exhibits include What the Buzz (an exhibition where your children can learn all about the honeybee). Weis Market (children can shop in a store exhibit). A, B, & C Bank (children can learn about money). Take Flight (off they go in an A10 cockpit). Engine Co. No 5 (children drive a fire truck simulator and can dress in firefighter gear). Pet Vet (children explore pets and their care), and coming soon, Doctor Demtrak's Healthy You (with a focus on children's health). Last, the Kids Commons' addition was to fill a need for weekday preschool activities, summer camps, and weekend programming.

The Story Garden presents thirteen different areas that focus on reading. The garden provides a happy place where children can play and learn at the same time. Children can play with characters from a story at the Story Garden. they are reading by using their imagination. The garden encourages our young children to learn and develop a love for nature.

CHAPTER SEVEN

SPECIAL EVENTS IN BINGHAMTON

Each year, there are many special events in the area. The activities that we have enjoyed as a family the most would be the Spiedie Fest & Balloon Rally Expo, The LUMA Lights Festival, Dick's Sporting Goods Open, and the many parades we have here. The St. Patrick's Day Parade has been a family favorite for years!

Spiedie Fest? What is a spiedie? They marinate spiedies as cubes of meat placed on a skewer and then grilled over an open flame. Initially, the recipe comprised lamb meat, but now chicken, beef, and pork have become great substitutes. All right, well…… what is a Spiedie Fest?

Over thirty-five years ago, a few families in the Binghamton area all claimed to have the best spiedie recipe. Although this was friendly boasting, the only way to decide who had the best spiedie turned into a contest. The winner gets the boasting rights! And so, it was. They held the first Spiedie Fest cooking contests in 1983 and 1984.

After a successful event in 1984, a small committee formed and created the first SpiedieFest and Balloon Rally at Otsiningo Park. The gathering of friends introduced everyone's spiedie recipes, launched hot air balloons, featured local music, and created an area for the children to play. The new festival would be fun for the community to enjoy at a very affordable cost.

Four thousand people attended the first year of Spiedie Fest. Today, many consider our SpiedieFest to be one of the top hot-air balloon rallies in the country. Over three days, the event now draws over one hundred thousand people. That is quite a change after thirty-five years!

Spiedies Photo courtesy of Otsiningo Park

The SpiedieFest event now brings in actors, sports figures, entertainers, singers, and bands to entertain the large crowds. Many gather to watch the balloons go up, shop for many crafts, and enjoy a freshly made spiedie! Who has the best spiedie? You be the judge!

Balloons are launching over the crowds at Spiediefest!

Red, White, and Blue Balloon were going up, up, and away!

Spiediefest Balloon Rally is underway in Otsiningo Park.

Spiediefest Balloon Rally is underway in Otsiningo Park.

Spiediefest Balloon Rally is underway in Otsiningo Park.

Spiediefest Balloon Rally is underway in Otsiningo Park.

Spiediefest Balloon Rally is underway in Otsiningo Park.

Spiediefest Balloon Rally is underway in Otsiningo Park.

Spiediefest Balloon Rally is underway in Otsiningo Park.

Spiediefest Balloon Rally is underway in Otsiningo Park.

All the pictures are courtesy of Spiediefest & Balloon Rally

The Library of Congress honored with recognition the SpiedieFest with a Legacy Award in 2001. Presently a SpiedieFest display lives in the Library of Congress in Washington, D.C. The SpiedieFest received an award from the Syracuse Parks & Recreation as the Year's Event for New York State in the same year. In 2005, Destination Magazine named the SpiedieFest event in the 100 Destinations in the U.S. The Food Channel ran an episode on the SpiedieFest and Balloon Rally featuring the spiedie cooking contest and is still running today. Our local newspaper, the Press & Sun-Bulletin, named the SpiedieFest one of the top events in the Readers' Choice Awards every year since the contest began. Since SpiedieFest started, the event donated over one million dollars to great organizations and charities right here in our area.

Summer fun at the Spiediefest.

One festival that only takes place once a year and only in Binghamton, the LUMA Projection Lights Festival! The festival uses the beautiful architecture of downtown Binghamton that Isaac Parry and other architects designed long ago. Artists worldwide come to Binghamton and illuminate creative uses Downtown Binghamton's stunning architecture as its canvas. Their creations project with lighting using mapping designed for each specific building and bring them back to us presented in a new, beautiful way. One night show, the LUMA Lights Festival can get a crowd of over thirty thousand into downtown Binghamton's streets.

LUMA is a commitment to the arts in our area. It is a community event that involves our people, businesses, and city officials. A labor of love that benefits our city the LUMA Festival provides a cultural event that we can attend for free. Many visitors come to our area because of the event.

The LUMA Projection Arts Festival usually takes place in early September. It is the only city in the country that it appears in. LUMA's first show was in 2015 with three installations and had an audience estimated at twenty thousand.

The LUMA Projection Arts Festival focuses on large, building-scale illuminations using a projection mapping technique, with the city's architecture as the canvas. It is the largest such festival in the United States, focusing on this type of art. The festival has continued to grow each year. Many artists are now adding such elements of interactive media.

The festival is free to the public, with many thanks to our generous community sponsors who help make this possible.

LUMA built a virtual Crowd-Sourced Art Gallery, curated by local not-for-profit The Memory Maker Project, and exposing dozens of local emerging artists to twenty-five thousand visitors.

Crowds gathering at the LUMA Lights Festival!

The festival has hosted a competition for emerging artists, with a $5000 prize for the winning artist.

More great examples of the LUMA projection festival!

The Binghamton Philharmonic and LUMA worked together for a unique animated feature, exposing new listeners to classical music with a free performance.

More great examples of the LUMA projection festival!

Every LUMA festival highlights the unique talents of the many professionals living in our community. Binghamton's reputation is growing as a revitalized community with many excellent skills and attractions for visitors to enjoy.

New illusions produced every year create the effect that the buildings are changing their physical structure. LUMA also adds vital elements to the mapped projections, such as orchestral music, motion-captured actors, and audience interactivity. This atmosphere encourages visitors to walk the festival at their own comfortable pace.

LUMA Festival estimated one-night economic impact is $900,000.

More great examples of the LUMA projection festival!

More great examples of the LUMA projection festival!

Throughout the year, LUMA offers free projection mapping classes for emerging artists in the region.

More great examples of the LUMA projection festival!

More great examples of the LUMA projection festival!

More great examples of the LUMA projection festival!

All the mapped projections used come from both international and local artists. Previous LUMA installations have included work with internationally recognized artists, such as the debut of the first 3D animation of characters from the BC (comic strip) with contained work from Mason Mastroianni.

The Dick's Sporting Goods Open is a PGA Tour Champions golfing event in Endicott, New York. It debuted in July 2007, replacing the previous PGA Tour Event called the BC Open. Dick's Sporting Goods sponsors the event, which originated their business in Binghamton with their very first store.

The tournament takes place at the En-Joie Golf Club in Endicott. En-Joie Golf Club opened ninety-three years ago in 1927. George F. Johnson created the golf course as a recreation place for his employees at the local shoe factory in Endicott. Michael Hurdzan renovated the golf course layout in 1998-99 by changing the original relatively flat, round greens into huge, undulating greens that challenge all golfers' levels. With narrow, tree-lined fairways coupled with large, elevated greens, the En-Joie golf course is a real test for golfers of all skill levels.

2014 Champion Bernhard Langer, photo courtesy of Dick's Sporting Goods Open.

2019-World Golf Hall of Fame Member Fred Couples.

The 2019 Concert featured Keith Urban, Concert on the Green, Both photos courtesy of Dick's Sporting Goods Open.

Every golf tournament includes a special concert event. Keith Urban, Tim McGraw, and Bon Jovi have entertained crowds throughout the years.

CHAPTER EIGHT

SPECIALTY FOODS AND RESTAURANTS

SPIEDIES!!

Well, now we hit on a subject near and dear to my heart, FOOD! It well known the Binghamton area for the spiedie sandwich (one slice of Italian bread from a skewer). The names for spiedies come from the Italian word spiedo, which translated means kitchen cooking spit. Spiedies originated with the Italian Binghamton immigrant population way back in the 1920s. An Endicott restaurateur, Augustine Iacovelli, helped make them famous by introducing them to his restaurant in 1939. He called his original sauce Zuzu, and it comprised wine vinegar, wine, lemon juice, garlic, and mint. Originally made from lamb, now we use different meats and marinades. We even have a couple of local marinades available in a bottle from Salamida and Lupo's.

Another restaurant has been offering spiedies since 1993. At one point, they were averaging two thousand five hundred pounds of cooked and raw spiedies in a week! They tailored their menu around Spiedie specialties thus developed a gourmet style Spiedie.

Stop in and try their SPIEDISSIMO™ gourmet Spiedie or some St. Louis style Ribs. Burgers, steaks, and salads round out their menu that includes several popular sides.

Enjoy our local food that Binghamton is famous for. We have a couple of restaurants who grille up the most delicious spiedies. Lupo's S&S Char-Pit has been serving up spiedies since 1951.

Experience Spiedies the original way with marinated lamb or try them using chicken or pork. Any way they are all delicious. Lupo's offers a menu featuring subs, salads, sandwiches, combos, and a good selection of sides. You can find Lupo's Spiedies in just about every supermarket in the Binghamton area as well. Become your own chef on your outdoor grille.

There are so many great restaurants in the Binghamton area, which makes this hard for me. These are my favorites, and all are a piece of the puzzle why I never moved. I am Italian, so this may have influenced my choices.

I have lived in Binghamton my entire life. For the last fifty-seven years, I made my home on the east side. This side of the city is not what it used to be. but most cities can make the same claim. However, being an Italian in ethnicity I always gravitated towards Italian food. Nestled on the east side of Binghamton are two very good Italian restaurants.

Cortese restaurant began serving delicious Italian meals in the year of 1947. The restaurant is still standing tall after serving the public for seventy-five years now. The Cortese family still runs the restaurant to this very day.

Cortese offers a wide variety of appetizers, several delicious veal and chicken dishes, and a wide selection of their famous Italian specialties. They make sauce and pasta on the premises fresh every day.

That is not all. They also serve beef and pork varieties and suggest you order their pork chops, steaks, and prime ribs, "Milanese style." A Cortese exclusive passed on from generations. Cortese offers a good selection of seafood, including surf and turf.

If you are not in the mood for a special meal, Cortese offers many ideas including, salads, submarine sandwiches, wraps, basket dinners and a full sandwich menu. Cortese also makes delicious pizza to eat in or take out along with everyone's favorite chicken wings.

The restaurant offers a very comfortable friendly atmosphere for you to enjoy a meal and has added a beautiful outdoor seating area for their customers' enjoyment. Make it a priority to stop at Cortese restaurant on Robinson Street on your next visit.

Michelangelo's offers fantastic Italian food and excellent pizza!

Another great restaurant thrives on the east side of Binghamton. If you like Italian food, this is a must stop location. A couple of Italian restaurateurs started years ago in the Oakdale Mall with a popular location by the name of Villa Pizza. After a few years of success, they moved to a new location on the east side and Michaelangelo's Pizzeria and Ristorante were born. Well known for great food this restaurant withstood not one, but two floods. The restaurant came back from these setbacks in grand style, making many improvements.

You can eat-in or take out and offer lunch specials every day. Many choices of appetizers including their popular Garlic Knots. Many entrees to choose from made with chicken, veal, pork chops and steak. My favorite is Chicken Parmesan. If you are looking for another mouthwatering entrée, try their Braciole Alla Barese. They feature such specialties such as Chicken Marsala, Greek Chicken, Steak Marsala, Stuffed Sole and various soups, and salads.

Michaelangelo's features a full array of Italian pasta or Pasta with Seafood dishes. Calzones and delicious Pizza that make its way to our home often. All their sauces are gluten-free. If you are in the mood for a submarine sandwich, they offer a variety of hot and cold choices. Do not forget dessert, try their favorites, including Tiramisu or an Italian favorite, Cannoli! If you visit Binghamton for an event, Michaelangelo's caters too!

If you love Italian food, Binghamton has another long-standing family-run restaurant in the center of the city. Since 1946, Little Venice has been serving delicious Italian food for all to enjoy. As a young boy, I can remember going through the corner door of their original location to pick up food for our family.

Then, the restaurant was at the corner of Court and Cherry Street, until they had the misfortune of a fire that ultimately led them to their current location. I have vivid memories of that fire as we lived right next door to the restaurant on Cherry Street. Little Venice is in its seventy-fourth years of business and a staple of our city.

Little Venice offers a wide variety of lunch choices, including their number one bestseller, freshly made Spaghetti with their famous Meat Logs. They make pasta and Sauce fresh in the house every day. Entrees featuring Veal, Chicken and Seafood. Look over their selection of House Specialty Parms and of course, Pizza. I have enjoyed the Meat Lovers Pizza. Delicious! You can "Create Your Own Pasta" which gives you the choice of pasta (from a choice of five), choose your sauce (from a choice of five), and choose your own toppings (from a choice of six)!

Little Venice has a wide selection of appetizers, house made soups, sandwiches, salads, and egg rolls. Little Venice offers a warm and inviting atmosphere and features over one hundred and fifty original signed paintings that surround you. Their sauce is so popular you can purchase a jar in their onsite or online store. Do not miss the Italian heritage the city of Binghamton offers.

We know the east side of Binghamton for its fine Italian restaurants. However, we have an Irish Pub and Restaurant that has been doing business here since 1922. The House of Reardon is a must stop location and the oldest Irish pub in the Binghamton area. Robert Norris is the president of the family-run restaurant. The House of Reardon is the place to go for an enjoyable meal or just relaxing with friends for a drink.

The House of Reardon offers lunch and dinner specials and a full menu, including Soups, Salads, Chicken Wings, Pierogies, Pizzas, Deli-Style Sandwiches, Wraps and Quesadillas with toppings. Must try's include their Pretzel Log with Honey Mustard or Cheese Sauce,

Garlic Chicken Wings, Poppy's Supreme Eight-piece Pizza including Your Choice of Five Toppings, Potato or Meat filled Pierogies and a large variety of mouthwatering Sandwich selections.

Are you ready for an Irish drink? How about a nice cold Guinness? House of Reardon states the Irish traditional message about the beverage on their menu. Sláinte! In an Irish pub, patrons toast each other sláinte (pronounced "slaan-sha") as they clink glasses of Guinness. Derived from the Old Irish adjective slán (which means "safe"), sláinte literally translates as "health" and stated as a stand-in for the more time-consuming "I drink to your health!" It's time for a toast at the House of Reardon.

The House of Reardon also has a four-season pavilion that can host large groups of people and an outdoor deck and bistro area used for parties. Whether you are inside or outside the House of Reardon, one thing you can count on is having a fun and enjoying experience.

Another fine Italian restaurant, New York Pizzeria, has just about any kind of pizza you could ask for besides fine Italian cuisine. One of the best places for pizza in Binghamton. If you are looking for a gourmet pizza, look no further than New York Pizzeria! Stop by to see the unique pizzas of the day. You will look like a kid in a candy store!

New York Pizzeria has become one of the most loved pizzerias in our area. How have they accomplished this? Building relationships with their customers and becoming an active member of our community. Privately owned, they have been making gourmet pizzas for over ten years now. They only have one thing in mind and that is creating a comfortable atmosphere for their customers to enjoy.

Just to name some of the long list of gourmet pizzas, stop in to try their Chicken Spiedie Pizza, Chicken Bacon Ranch Pizza, or the Chefs Special Pizza. The flavor will not disappoint. Tasty Italian dinner dishes, soups, salads, hot and cold subs, chicken wings, stuffed pizza, calzones, and Stromboli round out their delicious menu. Top off your meal with dessert and enjoy their Cannoli.

New York Pizzeria is just another shining example of the strong Italian heritage in Binghamton.

A great addition to the downtown Binghamton restaurant scene is PS Restaurant. PS has been serving French, Thai cuisine for over thirty-five years. They carry a wine list that has grown to over four hundred selections. PS Restaurant continues to win the Wine Spectator award for excellence. Their chef has won many awards throughout the years, including the Chef of the Year Southern Tier Chapter of the American Culinary Federation. In preparing their food, the term "fresh is best" describes it best. PS Restaurant cares about our area and is the founder of a website called www.stir-local.com. The website created a place for restaurants to go to inform the public of their specialties.

PS Restaurant whisks you away from Binghamton in your mind by offering the flavors of global cuisine. Enjoy Thai cuisine, French cuisine, Italian cuisine, and other Continental dishes right from the comfort of your table. Complete with a selection of wines to complement your meal. It will give you the feeling that you are there.

PS offers a variety of appetizers, including PS Wrapped Shrimp and Impossible Fritters. They also offer delicious soups and fresh salads. Their list of entrees is bursting with flavor, including Orange Horseradish Crusted Lobster Tail and Thai Roast Duck.

No meal is complete without dessert. They have a flavorful selection including Peanut Butter Chocolate Pie. After dinner, enjoy making a choice from a list of Dessert Wines or a three ounce pour of their Port • Sherry • Favorites. If coffee is your thing enjoy a Baileys Coffee or Peppermint Patty from their selections of coffee drinks.

PS Restaurant also caters on or off premise and has provided gourmet catering for over twenty years.

The Water Street Brewing Company is another place in Binghamton that is well worthy of the trip. It is the first modern brewery in the city and offers a variety of choices, including German Pilsners, Hefeweizens, hazy NEIPAs, barrel-aged stouts, and more. The business started in 2011 and is still going strong with dedicated owners and a head brewer that enjoys his craft.

Water Street Brewing Company

The Water Street Brewing Company offers a food menu with seasonal favorites like Chili Cheese Fries. Soups and salads and a variety of starters, such as loaded fries. Completing the list are a selection of burgers, sandwiches, and pub fare items. The restaurant offers a Sunday Brunch and weekday specials. They can hold special events onsite with proper notice.

Craft

In the center of the city, we have another restaurant gem. Craft Bar and Kitchen shines with a large selection of beer on tap and proudly presents a tasty list of sliders. Try the Craft slider, Shrimp slider or the Dubbel Decker slider, all included in their long list for your eating pleasure. The Craft is famous in our city for making mouthwatering milkshakes unlike any other. Do you like chocolate? Try their Binghamton Blackout shake. You will not be sorry.

The Craft also offers a variety of salad bowls and a tasty group of snacks and sides that will satisfy your hunger. They have a large amount of beer on tap, twenty-four varieties to be exact, and offer sixteen different canned flavors. That is not all. Ask to see their cocktail list, punch bowl items and wine list. Above all, this restaurant offers a great atmosphere inside and out when the weather is right.

Garage Taco Bar

Innovation is turning a gas station into a fine restaurant destination serving up fun and fantastic food. Binghamton has just that in the downtown area. The Garage Taco Bar offers relaxing dining inside and out, keeping their customers coming back for more.

Garage Taco Bar offers a wide selection of starters, several taco meals, many single tacos, Burritos and Quesadillas to satisfy anyone's appetite. Desserts feature the Horchata Churros and Sopopillia.

Outside dining is an experience sitting alongside the beautiful painted mural on the building next door. They offer all this and give you the opportunity to purchase a souvenir t-shirt of bottle of their hot sauce on the way out. Just another great dining experience in downtown Binghamton.

The Lost Dog Cafe

The Lost Dog Café and Lounge. Wow, where do I start? Let us begin by saying this historic building was once a cigar factory. Back in the day, Binghamton manufactured cigars, and the only city that produced more was New York City! If that is not fascinating enough, imagine three local girls that formed a band and headed out to New York City for fame and fortune. After spending some time there, they eventually came back home. When in NYC and need a place to relax, they visited many cafes? At the time there were no cafes here, so what could be better?

Special events take place here, and if you like Jazz, this is the place to go. So, if you want a comfortable place to relax, enjoy good food, not to mention great coffee, The Lost Dog Café is your best bet. While there, ask them how they got their name!

Burger Mondays, a part of the State Street-Henry Street Historic District that still functions as a great restaurant in downtown Binghamton. Formerly the Binghamton Republican-Herald building. Enjoy an excellent meal in the atmosphere once a historic newspaper building has become a popular restaurant called Burger Mondays Bar & Grille! If you are in the mood for a mouth-watering made-from-scratch burger and fries, you have found a home at this beautiful restaurant.

Burger Mondays Bar & Grille opened in 2011 and describe their menu as fine dining on a bun. Fresh meat, hand-patted combined with house made sauces and served with fresh hand cut fries and a house made pickle.

Try the popular Classic Burger, Philly Cheese Steak Egg Rolls, Calamari Salad, Ahi Tuna Burger, or the Delmonico Steak. Executive Chef has a favorite called, "The Jonesy." Burger Mondays caters as well, including weddings and private parties both on and off site.

Burger Monday's

One of Binghamton's' popular Southside restaurants is the South City Publick House. The restaurant is in the old Kunkel building. They feature soups, salads, an array of sandwiches, burgers, and dinner specials. If you are in the mood to hear a band, this is the place to go.

SouthCity Publick House

Another restaurant in downtown Binghamton is Alexanders Café. Business people get away from their computers and stop into Alexander's for a needed break. Breakfast, lunch, early dinners feature Panini's, wraps, breakfast sandwiches, salads, homemade sides, and sweet ending desserts.

Alexanders Cafe

Proclaimed as an Internet cafe and a restaurant hot spot. Breakfast, lunch, or dinner, they have a menu bursting with flavor. Alexander's Cafe offers milkshakes, smoothies, salads, wraps, sandwiches, ice cream, sundaes, homemade macaroni, and potato salads. Binghamton customers have developed a special love for their Signature Sandwiches.

Between two of Binghamton's Historic districts, inside the Kilmer Building is another excellent downtown restaurant named Remliks Grille and Oyster Bar. Remlik spelled backward is Kilmer.

What a great way to honor an old building from the past. The building transformed from Swamp root to distinctive dining. Enjoy their comfortable atmosphere with a menu that includes soups, salads, fantastic appetizers, and dinner selections. Do not forget sushi and their raw bar as well.

Remnick's Oyster Bar & Grille

Remlik's Oyster Bar & Grille offers fine dining in the historical Kilmer Building. Binghamton native Anthony Yanuzzi became executive chef about ten years ago and has brought years of experience and training to the restaurant. His specialty is homemade Italian cooking and the discipline of French Cuisine.

Are you looking for a great bakery or deli? How about the one that I grew up with, Di Rienzo Bros. Deli Bakery! They have only been open since 1904! If you are looking for a hot loaf of uncut

Italian bread, fresh hard rolls, or a sheet of incredible pizza, this is the place to go. It is also a favorite stop for fried fish during Lent, trays of Italian meats and cheeses, and Italian cookies. DiRienzo's Bakery & Deli is a business formed in the year 1904 by an Italian immigrant named Gaetano DiRienzo and still stands today! Still using the original recipe for their fresh bread, they started the bakery with. In the eighties, they began the business of selling fried fish. Their fried haddock has become a local legend. Lines form out the door every Friday and during Lent, the lines get even longer.

If you are looking for a unique and unforgettable bar and dining experience while in Binghamton. Look no further than the 205

DRY Bar and Restaurant. When you enter the door, you face a wall filled with books. Within this old bookcase is a hidden door that will bring you back in time as soon as you open it. You are now standing in an authentic 1920s Speakeasy.

They feature a list of appetizers, including Spicy Pickle Fries. Salads and Bowls including the Cat's Meow Salad, and Bigger Plate selections including The 205, and the Prohibition Burger. 205 DRY offers a selection of Cocktails, Seasonal Innovation's such as the Soul Mate, and 205 Classics including the 205's Old Fashioned. They even have a secret shots menu available upon request. Enjoy your trip back in time at 205 DRY.

205 Dry

Peterson's Tavern. They are a small tavern with great food that is big on flavor. Feature an outdoor patio for relaxation in warmer weather. We know Petersons Tavern for excellent steaks, traditional American and Italian cuisines. This tavern also provides live music as well.

Peterson's Tavern has a beautiful mural on the building's side, float like a butterfly, sting like a Bee!

What makes Peterson's Tavern so popular? We have voted for them as the best new bar in Binghamton! They have award winning food items, an outstanding outdoor patio, incredible specialty cocktails and live music weekly. Complete menu includes a selection of burgers, chicken wings, soups, salads, spiedies, quesadillas, Mac and cheese and Prime Rib. Peterson's offers daily and weekend specials and is located right across the street from a historical landmark.

Social on State restaurant has a special way for you to enjoy your dining experience. It is a sharing experience, and the menu comprises tapas dishes made to order. They deliver the food to your table throughout your dining experience.

Their menu lists a variety of small plates with delicious choices such as Lobster Mac and Cheese or Arugula Barrata Salad just to name a couple. Large Plate selections include Atlantic Salmon or Steak & Lobster among others. If you enjoy sharing your food in a great social atmosphere, this is for you.

Social on State

Another favorite spot nestled on Washington Street is Binghamton Hots. The menu includes lunch and dinner items such as homemade soups, salads, wraps, hot plates, subs, sandwiches, hot dogs, spiedies, and burgers. Vegan and vegetarian options are also on their menu. Great restaurant for late-night service, open late six nights a week.

Try their specialty, the classic Rochester Garbage Hot Plate that comprises your choice of meat, two sides and Martins Potato Roll covered with their own homemade "Rochester Style Hot Sauce."

Binghamton Hots

Another location I supported as a child is still going strong right in the middle of downtown Binghamton. M&D R-NUTS has been serving Binghamton in premium quality nuts and fruits for over seventy years. We guarantee freshness by cooking the nuts in small quantities. Besides the variety of nuts, M&D has a large selection of candy, chocolates, fruits, and tray options.

M&D-R-NUTS

The Spot Restaurant has been serving up delicious meals for the last forty-nine years. I used to stop at the diner for breakfast many times. The restaurant specializes in Greek food dishes. The Spot has a lengthy lunch and dinner menu. From burgers to salads, seafood to pastas or a juicy steak the selections of fresh food seem never ending.

The biggest task is trying to move away from the display case featuring their fresh baked items and treats. I have always had a problem doing that! Also proudly displayed is their famous cheesecake, that is a perfect ending to a delicious meal.

The Spot Diner Restaurant

If breakfast is your thing another stop on Washington Street would make Strange Brew a priority stop. They offer breakfast all day long and offer a variety of freshly brewed coffee proudly roasted locally from another Binghamton born business, Java Joes Roasting

Company. Breakfast menu includes hand crafted breakfast sandwiches, omelets, made to order oatmeal, and Fruit Parfaits.

Strange Brew also has a lunch menu with tasty pressed sandwiches, fresh n salads, house made soups, their signature gourmet Mac and cheese, and customer favorite grilled Mac and cheese sandwiches.

The Strange Brew

The Park Diner has been a Binghamton favorite since 1967. A complete menu to choose from, they take pride in the freshness of their food and friendly service. The diner has spectacular views overlooking the Susquehanna River.

A popular spot for breakfast, lunch and dinner serving breast of chicken, steaks, chops, deli sandwiches, triple decker sandwiches, salads, platters, appetizers, burgers, seafood, and Italian dishes. The Park Diner has daily specials and I suggest you try one of their gyros.

The Park Diner

CHAPTER NINE

BINGHAMTON SPORTS AND ENTERTAINMENT!

Broome County owns and operates The Visions Federal Credit Union Veterans Memorial Arena (formerly the Broome County Veterans Memorial Arena) and the Broome County Forum Theatre.

The Visions Federal Credit Union Veterans Memorial Arena is a five-thousand-seat arena. It is home to the Binghamton Black Bears of the Federal Prospects Hockey League. The Arena anchors the downtown area as a center for various sports, concerts, expos, and family events.

Outside of the Arena is a beautiful place of honor for our veterans.

The construction of the Arena took place in 1973 with a design resulting from a nationwide competition. Some of the top stars in the world have played the Arena. The first act at the Arena was the Barnum & Bailey circus in May 1973. Chicago played the first concert at the Arena with Bruce Springsteen as the opener.

Along with professional baseball, Binghamton has maintained a passion for professional hockey. Our first team, Broome Dusters, started the puck rolling back in 1973. The team was part of the NAHL from 1973 to 1977 when the league folded. A classic game against Syracuse became the main focal point for the movie called "Slapshot!" The game in question dished out 192 penalty minutes. The game provided more fighting than actual hockey. Fighting began before the game even started when Syracuse player Bill Goldthorpe confronted players in pre-game warmups while still in civilian clothes. Who can forget his blond Afro?

The next team formed to play here was the Binghamton Dusters, and they added the team into the AHL. The Binghamton Dusters existed from 1977 to 1980.

This paved the way to our next team, the Binghamton Whalers one level below the Hartford Whalers in the NHL. For the next ten years, the Binghamton Whalers had a fair amount of success but never won a championship. Hartford sold the franchise to the New York Rangers last year.

The result was the addition of our next team, the Binghamton Rangers. From 1990 to 1997, the Rangers played in our arena and had great success. They won a regular season title and four divisional titles. The last year was unsuccessful, and the Rangers moved the franchise to Hartford, CT.

Thus, it was time for our next hockey team, the BC Icemen. Local cartoonist Johnny Hart created their logo. The team was part of the United Hockey League from 1997 to 2002. The BC Icemen won two divisional championships during their time here. Eventually, the team sold to an investor in the year 2001.

The new owner went bankrupt and a new group stepped with a team in the AHL, and the Binghamton Senators came into existence. The Senators would have the longest time playing in the arena from 2002 to 2017. They won a Calder Cup Championship in 2011, but for most of their time spent here gave a subpar performance. After the last season, Ottawa moved the franchise to a different location.

The New Jersey Devils of the NHL were looking for a place to move their team playing in Albany. Binghamton was a good fit, so the team moved here. The Binghamton Devils were born and played hockey in the Arena until 2021 when the Devils moved the franchise to Utica.

Things were not looking good for a hockey team here. However, a new owner stepped in and formed a new team in the Federal Prospects Hockey League. Our new team became the Binghamton Black Bears. Binghamton is a hockey town and we support every team with enthusiasm.

Who's Performed at our Arena?

3 Doors Down, AC/D.C., Adam Ant, Aerosmith, Air Supply, Alabama, Alan Jackson, Alice Cooper, Allman Brothers Band, America, American Idol XIV, Angel, Andrew Dice Clay, Avicii, B.B. King, Barenaked Ladies, Barry Manilow, U.S. Senator Bernie Sanders (presidential candidate), Bill Gaither, Billy Ray Cyrus, Black Sabbath, Blackhawk, Blue Öyster Cult, Bob Dylan, Bob Hope, Bob Seger & The Silver Bullet Band, Bobby Vinton, Bon Jovi, Boyz II Men, Brantley Gilbert, Bro Safari, Brooks & Dunn, Bruce Springsteen, Bryan Adams, Buckcherry, Cab Calloway, Candlebox, Captain & Tennille, Carrie Underwood, Casting Crowns, Celtic Thunder, Charlie Pride, Cheap Trick, Cher, Chevelle, Chicago, Conway Twitty, Count Basie, Crosby, Stills, Nash & Young, Darius

Rucker, Daughtry, David Copperfield, David Lee Roth, Dave Matthews Band, Def Leppard, Diana Ross, Dick Clark, Dierks Bentley, Dire Straits, Disney On Ice, Dolly Parton, Don Henley, Doobie Brothers, Dru Hill, Eddie Murphy, Edgar Winter Group, Electric Light Orchestra, Elton John, Elvis Presley, Emerson, Lake & Palmer, Engelbert Humperdinck, Eric Church, Eric Clapton, Faith Hill, Faster Pussycat, Fleetwood Mac, Foreigner, Frank Sinatra, Frank Zappa, Furthur, Garth Brooks, Gary Lewis and The Playboys, Gary Puckett and the Union Gap, Genesis, George Jones, George Thorogood and The Delaware Destroyers, Glen Campbell, Godsmack, Goo Goo Dolls, Gov't. Mule, Grateful Dead, Green Day, Gretchen Wilson, Hall & Oates, Harlem Globetrotters, Harry Chapin, Heart, Hinder, Howie Mandel, Huey Lewis and the News, Ice Capades, Iron Maiden, Jackson Browne, James Taylor, Jeff Dunham, Jerry Lee Lewis, Jethro Tull, Jimmy Buffett, Joan Baez, John Cougar Mellencamp, John Denver, John Fogerty, Johnny Cash, Johnny Winter, Judas Priest, Kansas, KC and the Sunshine Band, Keith Sweat, Kelly Clarkson, Kenny G, Kenny Rogers, Kiss, Korn, Larry the Cable Guy, Liberace, Liza Minnelli, Lonestar, Loretta Lynn, Lorrie Morgan, Loverboy, Luke Bryan, M.C. Hammer, Marshall Tucker Band, Meatloaf, Megadeth, Melissa Etheridge, Mercy Me, Meshuggah, Metallica, Molly Hatchet, Moody Blues, Mötley Crüe, Muddy Waters, Natalie Merchant, Neil Diamond, Neil Sedaka, Newsboys, Nightranger, Orleans, Outlaws, Ozzy Osbourne, Paul

Anka, Papa Roach, Phish, Poison, Pretty Lights, Primus, Pure Prairie League, Queensrÿche, Rainbow, REO Speedwagon, Randy Travis, Ratt, Reba McEntire, Richard Marx, Rick Derringer, Ringling Bros. Circus, Rob Zombie, Robert Goulet, Robert Plant, Roberta Flack, Rod Stewart, Rodney Dangerfield, Royal Hanneford Circus, Rush, Sammy Hagar, Santana, Sarah Vaughan, Sawyer Brown, Scorpions, Sha Na Na, Shinedown, Sly & the Family Stone, Staind, Stars On Ice, Steve Green, Steve Martin, Stevie Wonder, Stone Temple Pilots, Sugarland, Sweet, Talking Heads, Ted Nugent, Ten Years After, The Beach Boys, The Black Crowes, The Carpenters, The Flaming Lips, The Go-Gos, The Kinks, The Lettermen, The Lipizzaner Stallions, The Monkees, The Muppets, The Pointer Sisters, The Statler Brothers, The Wiggles, Third Eye Blind, Three Dog Night, Tim McGraw, Toby Keith, Tom Jones, Tom Petty and the Heartbreakers, Tonic, Tony Bennett, Tony Orlando, Tool, Toto, Traffic, Trans-Siberian Orchestra, Twisted Sister, Uriah Heep, Van Halen, Vanilla Ice, Vic Damone, Vince Gill, Wayne Newton, Whitesnake, Willie Nelson, WWE, Yes, Yngwie J. Malmsteen, ZZ Top.

The Broome County Forum Theatre contains a historical past. The building is a performing arts theater with seating for 1,500 people and is our answer to Broadway in Binghamton. The Tri-Cities Opera and the Binghamton Philharmonic perform in The Forum as well. Concerts, comedians, conventions, and talent contests are some events hosted by the Forum. Robert Morton Theatre Organ is at the Forum.

In 1919, the original building became the Binghamton Theatre, which hosted silent and vaudeville acts. Because of introducing the film with sound and the harmful effects of the Depression. The Binghamton Theatre closed in 1931. In 1946, the new owners refurbished the facility and reopened it as a movie theatre. However, it closed again in 1951. Then, in 1960, after another significant renovation, the facility opened as the Capri Theatre. The Capri Theater closed in 1973.

Shortly after that, a local nonprofit group, the Tri-Cities Opera Workshop, organized to develop the Capri Theater into a performing arts theatre. The group intended to renovate the facility and then turn it over to Broome County Government for operation. In 1975, the Broome County Legislature passed a resolution to accept the Capri

Theater's gift and run it as a performing arts theatre. That was the year that the Forum Theatre was born.

In 1975, the County built a dressing room addition. The building underwent another renovation in 1981 with the addition of a lobby and Recital Hall. Most recently, in 2011, the Forum received a complete seat replacement. The Wall of Stars displayed the stars from our area and found in the lobby area of The Forum. Today, the Forum Theatre continues to thrive as a center of arts and entertainment for the greater Binghamton area.

Who's Performed at The Forum?

Ani DiFranco, Brenda Lee, Brian Regan, Bryan Adams, Cabinet, Carlos Mencia, Celtic Woman, Chuck Mangione, David Sedaris,

Dopapod, Gabriel Iglesias, Gary Lewis, and the Playboys, George Carlin, Gordon Lightfoot, Henry Rollins, Jay Siegel's Tokens, Jerry Seinfeld, Jim Brickman, Kevin James, Lewis Black, Lisa Lampanelli, Lou Christie, Martina McBride, Maureen Hancock, moe., Natalie Merchant, Newsboys, Ray Davies, Riverdance, Robert Cray, Suzanne Vega, U.S. Senator Ted Cruz (presidential candidate interview w/ Sean Hannity), Tedeschi Trucks Band, The Fresh Beat Band, The Happenings, The Oak Ridge Boys, The Toys, Trey Anastasio Band, Umphrey's McGee.

The Tri-Cities Opera

Tri-Cities Opera has been the cultural centerpiece of the Southern Tier of New York for seventy years. Founded in 1949 by Peyton Hibbitt and the late Carmen Savoca, this regional opera company enjoys an exceptional reputation in the opera world for its Resident Artist Training Program, beautiful sets and costumes, and outstanding opera productions.

Tri-Cities Opera's main function is to produce professional quality opera using the talents of young artists. The Tri-Cities Opera sets a high standard for artistic excellence. They do this by demonstrating their devotion through the power of live musical storytelling.

Their Resident Artist Program provides talented young singers selected through a competitive audition process. This process provides the opportunity for the singers to learn the discipline of opera through performance of leading roles in major productions.

Their students perform at the Forum Theater and include main stage productions there. They also provide opportunities for smaller productions at the Clinton Street Opera Center.

Their Opera-Go-Round program is the self-supporting educational touring arm of Tri-Cities Opera and reaches over seventeen thousand young students with age-appropriate musical programs. Opera-Go-Round is often a child's first exposure to live musical storytelling.

The National Board of Directors of Opera America has honored Tri-Cities Opera, has received the President's Medal from Binghamton University, and has awarded the prestigious New York State Council on the Arts Governor's Award.

One thing I always enjoyed about Binghamton is the city's dedication to America's pastime. Baseball! In the late 1800s, they entertained us with the talent from the Binghamton Bingos. That team also played as the Binghamton Crickets for a couple of seasons. The early baseball was in action until the year 1925.

One player on the Binghamton Bingos, John W. "Bud Fowler" Jackson Jr. would become known as the first black professional baseball player. He played seventy years before Jackie Robinson and committee vote inducted him into Cooperstown Baseball Hall of Fame Class of 2022.

He played with the Binghamton Bingos in 1886. Fowler played 34 games with the Bingos posting a .350 batting average. His time with the team ended in the summer of 1887 after 9 Bingos players signed a petition threatening to quit if the team did not remove the two black players from the roster. Two weeks after his release the minor leagues agreed to ban black players. Bud played baseball in twenty-two different states and Canada as a pitcher and a second baseman and he never wore a glove! His baseball career lasted almost twenty years.

However, baseball was in our blood, so another team was born in 1923, which would last for forty-five years. The Triple Cities Triplets were born and became a farm team with the New York Yankees. In 1968, the field had to be torn down to make way for the new highway Route 17.

John W. "Bud Fowler" Jackson Jr.

Three Champions Meet at Johnson Field

Joe DiMaggio and Lou Gehrig with George Johnson before a game in our field.

During those years, many Yankee greats visited our area for training and exhibition games. It thrilled us to see players like Lou Gehrig, Mickey Mantle and Joe DiMaggio in exhibition games and watched players grow into great talent such as Thurman Munson, Hall of Famer Whitey Ford and 1960 World Series MVP Bobby Richardson. The Triplets also had short affiliations with the Kansas City Athletics and the Milwaukee Braves.

After a twenty-year break, Binghamton was back in baseball with a brand-new stadium and a brand-new team. The Binghamton Mets took the field and became a member of the Eastern League. The team is a stepping stone on the way to the big show to become a New York Met in Major League Baseball.

A list of players who played in Binghamton and made it into the Major League include David Wright, Noah Syndergaard, Ike Davis, Michael Conforto, Jose Reyes, Jacob deGrom, Ruben Tejada, Edgardo Alfonzo, Pete Alonso, Brandon Nimmo, Steven Matz, Jay Payton, and Zack Wheeler.

The team is the Double AA Mets affiliate, but has undergone a name change. The team is now known as the Binghamton Rumble Ponies since 2016. On November 2021, the team has a new owner. They announced he has a twenty-three-year extension with the Double AA Mets. As part of the deal, 3.1 million dollars will upgrade the stadium to MLB standards. The stadium, now named Mirabito Stadium will be home to the Rumble Ponies until 2045.

Former owner invested nine million dollars a few years ago to modernize the stadium and make it fan friendly. New seats, hospitality sections and the installation of new video scoreboards. They added additional improvements for the players.

Binghamton baseball has always been community orientated. This picture is of a girls' softball team I coached. The Binghamton Mets allowed us to walk around the stadium with our French's Mustard costume. I was in sales back then for the R. T. French Company based in Rochester, and yes, I sold French's Mustard!

Mirabito Stadium, home to our Binghamton Rumble Ponies.

Mirabito Stadium and the entrance to Rumbletown.

Mirabito Stadium, Photo courtesy of the Rumble Ponies!

**The Anderson Center for the Performing Arts supplies
entertainment for the Binghamton area.**

Another great place we have enjoyed performances in
Binghamton is at the Anderson Center for the Performing Arts.

Binghamton University added The Anderson Center for the Performing Arts to its campus in 1985. Since that time, they have hosted performances that draw over one hundred thousand guests every year. Performances include world-renowned symphonies, University student soloists, pop and rock concerts, opera, ballet, dance troupes, and international theater.

The Anderson Center contains the Osterhout Concert Theater, which offers one hundred and seventy-seats and has retractable walls with sliding windows. That feature allows the theater to turn into an arena during the summer months and provides an additional one thousand five hundred seats for guests to enjoy performances from outside under the stars.

CHAPTER TEN

TWO GREAT UNIVERSITIES IN BINGHAMTON

To be honest, growing up in this area can even fulfill a need when choosing a college. I remember Binghamton University as Harpur College when I was a young man. However, Binghamton University has come a long way since that time. Binghamton University has over one hundred twenty buildings in our area and expands into the Vestal and Johnson City areas.

Officially, it is one of four State Universities of New York but is better known as Binghamton University. As of Fall 2018, almost eighteen thousand undergraduate and graduate students attend the university. The college opened in 1946 and has grown from a small liberal arts college into a large research university ranked in the top public colleges in the United States. Many compare the quality of education provided here to the colleges in the Ivy League.

The college buildings of this campus form the shape of a brain!

Binghamton University offers schools including Harpur College of Arts and Science, College of Community and Public Affairs, Decker School of Nursing, School of Management, Thomas J. Watson School of Engineering and Applied Science, The Graduate School, and The School of Pharmacy and Pharmaceutical Sciences.

Binghamton University was in the news this year as one of their professors won the 2019 Nobel Peace Prize. An incredible honor for M. Stanley Whittingham, a professor in chemistry and materials science and engineering. He won the award with John Goodenough from the University of Texas at Austin and Akira Yoshino from Meijo University in Japan. Their commitment and research led to the development of the lithium-ion battery. We will benefit from their work as the lithium-ion battery will enhance powerful, portable electronics and electric cars.

We know Binghamton University athletic teams as the "Bearcats." They compete in Division one of the National Collegiate Athletic Association as a member of the America East Conference.

Look no further, as we have a great university right here in Binghamton!

Beautiful new Events Center hosts university sporting events.

Our other college in the Binghamton area is one that I attended, graduating back in 1976. The college received the new name SUNY Broome Community College. The focus of education that they offer is on their main campus. However, they have some classes in Waverly, Owego, and within the city of Binghamton.

The school comprises fifteen buildings and has an enrollment of approximately six thousand students. New upgrades have finished on the athletic facilities such as the baseball fields, soccer and lacrosse fields, tennis courts, and the Dick Baldwin Gym. Dick Baldwin is the third-winningest basketball coach across two- and four-year colleges. I am proud to say that I was a part of the very first lacrosse team from Broome Community College. BCC has also recently added a new ice rink facility.

Besides those improvements, the college has also added a theater that hosts campus performances named The Little Theater. Also, another addition recently completed is the new student housing building. I am happy to be one of over forty-one thousand alumni from SUNY Broome Community College.

Student housing now at SUNY Broome.

Twilight on the campus of SUNY Broome Community College

CHAPTER ELEVEN

TRADITIONS FROM OUR PAST CONTINUE

There is nothing more traditional than a parade, and my family has attended more than their fair share of them. I think the most exciting event in Binghamton would have to be the Saint Patrick's Day Parade. The parade takes place every year here and has been around for over fifty years. It is the day that the city turns green. The Irish bars become even fully decorated in green, and the city workers also paint the lines in the street emerald green. The tradition starts with a mass at St. Mary's Church and fills the city streets afterward. I am Italian; however, my wife was very Irish (we lost her to cancer nine years ago). And my children follow suit with a strong Irish ancestry.

St. Patrick's Church has been around for a long time, built because of the massive Irish population we have in Binghamton. Can you guess who the architect was? Isaac G. Perry created another masterpiece. One thing that the Binghamton area always believed in was providing places to worship. I could not tell you how many churches we have in our city. Anyway, I think this is an excellent place for the parade to start. Parade day begins with a mass at St. Patrick's Church. The St. Patrick's Day Parade in Binghamton will enter the fifty-third year in 2020.

There is no better way to honor our Irish heritage that made this city great than the St. Patrick's Day Parade.

Binghamton's St. Patrick's Day Parade event dates to 1967, and has become an annual event growing in popularity every year. The "Hibernian Parade Committee," an Irish-Catholic heritage organization plans the parade each year.

Originally, it was a way to honor contributions of the Irish community here locally, specifically members of the police and fire departments. They planned the first parade in the basement of the St.

John's Catholic Church on Livingston Street. The original parade only featured a high school band and some marchers and only lasted about twenty minutes. Today, people come from miles away to see our parade, and the length has grown to over ninety minutes. In 2000, then-Texas Gov. George W. Bush walked in the parade during his campaign.

To secure these pipe bands for Binghamton's parade, the date needed to change so as not conflict with New York City's and other larger city's festivities. And while the parade is not on the actual holiday, it has flourished. The day begins with a Catholic mass at St. Mary of the Assumption on Fayette Street. After the parade, a post-parade party takes place at Seton Catholic High School, a popular event that features groups from the parade, including the pipe bands, food, and Irish vendors. This event is a large fundraiser for the parade.

Another event that takes place before the St. Patrick's Day Parade is the Belmar Parade Day Mile. The Belmar Parade Day Mile is a one-mile race down Main Street. in Binghamton. The race begins at the Broome County Public Library and ends at the Belmar Pub on Main Street.

July Fest is the next traditional festival and has been for fifty-eight years. July Fest is a three-day event held in downtown Binghamton that features all kinds of fun for every age. Binghamton draws many people from all over the east coast for this event.

It is time to enjoy quality art, crafts, food, and music. Highlights include a Music and Jazz Festival, Antique Car Show, Artists in Action (where you can learn, create, and browse art), the Parlor City 5K, and the Kidz Art Zone, as well as guidance for kids to make and take their arts & crafts. The July Fest event started back in 1962 and still runs strong today!

Another one-hundred-year-old plus tradition is the annual St. Mary of the Assumption Bazaar customarily held in August. This event welcomes the entire community to come together and enjoy a weekend of live music, delicious home-cooked food, drinks, games, and other activities. The bazaar will be St. Mary of the Assumption church's 107th year hosting this bazaar. The church held its first one in 1913 to celebrate Mary's Assumption into Heaven, which lies on August 15.

Friday and Saturday feature live music for all to enjoy. Sunday usually offers a cookout followed by their super raffle drawing. Some examples of the beautiful food at the bazaar include Homemade Pasta Fagioli, Tripe, Homemade Meatball Sandwiches, Spinach Sandwiches, Pepper and Egg Sandwiches, Sausage and Peppers, Steak Sandwiches, Grilled Pizza, Spiedies, Pizza Fritte, Cannoli, Pizzella, Italian Love Cake, Crispelles and more. I can still remember how I looked forward to this bazaar as a child, and one of my favorite foods that was available was butter beans. I loved those!

The newest tradition, called Porchfest, is an entirely free event and completely volunteer-driven. Porchfest is a music festival that takes place on the last Sunday of every August throughout the Abel Bennett Historic District neighborhoods in the heart of Binghamton's West Side.

Many neighborhood residents use their porches, steps, driveways, and yards as a stage to entertain passersby. These musicians get to spend the day playing their tunes for all to enjoy. It is common to see people dance; children build lemonade stands, and some neighbors even set up garage sales. Talk about a family and community event. Look no further than Porchfest!

Another tradition that I mentioned earlier in the book is the LUMA Projection Arts Festival in September. Binghamton is the only current city in the United States that has this festival.

This year marks the 19th annual Blues at the Bridge Festival. The event is a September music festival on the South Washington Street Bridge that draws big crowds each year. A quote from an organizer, Tom Martino says it all, "one reason it makes me happy doing this event is that many people who come here are, maybe unfortunate financially," Martinos said. "They get to come here and see great, great bands where it doesn't cost them a dime to come."

The best way to describe this event would be that it is a community day providing excellent music, lots of fun, beautiful places to shop, and lots of food. This event oozes with the family atmosphere and community spirit. Just imagine this whole idea started years ago when a bunch of friends wanted to get together to play some music on the South Washington Street bridge. Now, the event has expanded to include both the South Washington Street Bridge and the Memorial Bridge. People are now enjoying the festival from the Confluence Park area as well.

As we enter the month of October in Binghamton, it is now time for our annual Columbus Day Parade and Italian Festival. Again, a great way to honor the strong Italian heritage helped make this city a great place to live. Speaking for myself and as an Italian, I am proud that we maintain this event in Binghamton.

The parade starts with the raising of an Italian Flag outside the Binghamton City Hall. The annual Columbus Day Parade starts things off, followed by the Tournament of Marching Band Competition, and the Italian Festival entertains for the rest of the afternoon. The parade starts on Main Street and will cross the Court Street Bridge before finishing at the Broome County Courthouse. The Italian Festival takes place on Water Street and provides live music for all to enjoy.

I think this quote from our mayor Rich David says it all. "Year after year, Binghamton's Columbus Day festivities bring people of all ages from across the region to downtown to celebrate the culture, traditions, and accomplishments of our proud Italian-American community."

First Fridays are still going strong after sixteen years. A walking tour in downtown Binghamton highlights forty-five galleries that include open studios of artists and artisans, art exhibits and sales, restaurants, and shops. It is a three-hour event held on the first Friday of each month. Gorgeous Washington Street Association Sponsors First Friday's festivities.

Second Saturdays are a newer event held on the second Saturday of each month. Many businesses on Historic Clinton Street offer deals and other incentives to customers. We know Clinton Street as Antique Row. Many Clinton Street antique shops are offering their vintage and rare finds.

We know Binghamton for its bicycling and walking clubs, facilities, and trails. In 2007, Binghamton received the honor of the ninth-greenest city in the United States by *Country Home* magazine. Chenango River Trail, also known as the Chenango River Promenade, is a favorite spot in Binghamton. If water and greenery relax you, this is the place to go.

Start this journey by walking over to the South Washington Bridge that is impressive. The bridge is for pedestrian traffic only and one of the beautiful Historic landmarks we have in our city. Before you enter Confluence, Park read the engravings on "The Skirmisher," the statue honoring those before us.

Now you are entering Confluence Park, just a beautiful place to sit and reflect. Here you can see the merging of two rivers. The Susquehanna and the Chenango rivers combine here in this beautiful small park, highlighting the rivers and greenery. There is also a location to fish here, and if your timing is right, an excellent spot to watch the sunset.

From here, you can travel through the tunnel that will be the start of a walk along the Chenango River. Along the way, enjoy the greenery that surrounds you and the sun glistening off the surface of the water. It will not be long before you come upon the memorial to Martin Luther King and the Promenade made in his honor. It is a leisurely walk taking in different signs of nature that surround you.

The homes and businesses along the banks of the river can be an excellent capture for your camera.

Take in the sights and enjoy the fresh air as you continue the trail that measures in at one and a half miles. At the end of your walk, you enter the Cheri Lindsey Memorial Park, noticeable by the beautiful mural as you approach the park. The park is an excellent memorial to a wonderful little girl that used to play there. So, take the time to go to the park, sit on a bench, and enjoy the day.

In closing this book about my hometown, I have to say that I learned some things about the city that I love I did not know. It is hard to pinpoint one reason that I never desired to move away from here. I think this book touched on a lot of reasons. It seems like I hear someone saying that they dislike it here way too much. I believe in the freedom of speech, and if that is their opinion, that is fine. Thinking that other places do not have issues is just foolish. One other thing I hear is that there is nothing to do here. Are you kidding me!

I stayed in Binghamton because I believed in what all the others who came here before me stood for. The people cared about where they lived. They cared about people that worked for them; they cared about family life, these people cared about children, and they cared about faith. They created a feeling within me to stay here and carry the torch onward. They made a feeling that this was and is a great place to raise a family.

Those feelings continued as I thought it was best to be here for my parents as they grew older. Feelings continued within me as I married a local girl and wanted to be around her family as well. Now, I am here for my children and grandchildren, and I never regret raising my family here. If my wife Barbara were still here with us, she would say the same thing.

Home is where my heart is. My heart is in Binghamton, N.Y.!

PLEASE REVIEW MY BOOKS!

I am new to the art of becoming an author. Many have said that I wear my heart on my sleeve. That may be true, but I have always believed we should express ourselves the best way we can. Could you please take the small time necessary to help me in my new adventure by writing a short review of my books? I am always looking to improve my life in any way that I can. Leaving a book review, either good or bad, can only help me improve my writing.

Currently, Amazon has all my books available to purchase. Reviews help me get the message out to others with Amazon's

marketing tools. It is an easy process to leave a review there. Just go
to my Author Page: www.amazon.com/author/davidbogart

Website: www.dbbooks.us

Email: dbogart2@stny.rr.com

Thank you so much for your time!